# YOUR
# SERVICE
# SUCKS!

## ...AND YOUR COMPETITION
## LOVES YOU FOR IT

LeAnne Williamson & Victoria Bowring

# YOUR
# SERVICE
# SUCKS!

...AND YOUR COMPETITION
LOVES YOU FOR IT

LIFESUCCESS PUBLISHING, LLC
8900 E Pinnacle Peak Road, Suite D240
Scottsdale, AZ, 85255

| | |
|---|---|
| Telephone: | 800.473.7134 |
| Fax: | 480.661.1014 |
| E-mail: | admin@lifesuccesspublishing.com |
| ISBN: | 978-1-59930-284-3 |
| | |
| Cover: | Daniela Savone, LifeSuccess Publishing, LLC |
| Text: | Lloyd Arbour, LifeSuccess Publishing, LLC |
| | |
| Edit: | Publication Services |

COMPANIES, ORGANIZATIONS, INSTITUTIONS, AND INDUSTRY
PUBLICATIONS. Quantity discounts are available on bulk purchases of this book
for reselling, educational purposes, subscription incentives, gifts, sponsorship, or
fundraising. Special books or book excerpts can also be created to fit specific needs
such as private labeling with your logo on the cover and a message from a VIP
printed inside. For more information, please contact our Special Sales Department
at LifeSuccess Publishing, LLC.

# Dedication

To our families, who said we can do anything!

*friends* 🙂

*Live Wide Open!*

*Love ya Paul.*

# Acknowledgments

This book is the result of initiative and constant motivation. We would like to gratefully acknowledge Jeffrey Gitomer, Ken Blanchard, Ron Zemke, Kristin Anderson, Rockhurst University, and the International Customer Service Association. Much of what we have learned over the years came as the result of these individuals and organizations, all of which, in their own ways, inspired us through their tireless efforts in the field of customer hospitality. We have benefited from the teachings and advice of some of the very best.

In addition, we would like to acknowledge the countless individuals and companies we have worked with over the past several years. A little bit of each of them will be found here, weaving in and out of the pages.

Lastly, we would like to acknowledge each other. We have had the pleasure of sharing a stage and working with each other, which has taught us so much about ourselves. It is through our constant encouragement and support of each other that we have gained new insights about life and have been able to produce the first of many works on striving for excellence and reaching for the infinite potential in all of us.

# Contents

# Foreword

Now more than ever, the global economy and the Internet have given us the opportunity to serve more clients than in any other time in history. Unfortunately, this new age of business has also given way to impersonal customer hospitality. One of the primary reasons so many businesses fail today is due to poor or, in some cases, no customer hospitality. In any company, it is a necessity to build a loyal customer base. LeAnne's and Victoria's experience in the field of customer hospitality has taught them that businesses that are able to retain customers have a significant advantage over the competition.

Our ability to develop and maintain strong customer relationships defines our success. With all of the information available on the importance of this, why is it then that good customer hospitality is quickly becoming an oxymoron in today's fast-paced environment? The answer is simple: many fail to adequately train their employees, especially in today's economy. Each chapter in this book teaches you how to directly serve your customers and gives you all the necessary tools to go the extra mile and expand your customer base.

*Your Service Sucks* focuses on the single most important principle of customer hospitality—superior service leads to satisfied customers, which leads to better profits. Sadly, many companies don't realize that they are losing valuable customers by failing to exceed their customers' needs. Not only will poor customer hospitality cost you customers, but it will also create a negative image for your business through word of mouth. It's unfortunate that most businesses today don't realize how fast they are losing valuable customers. LeAnne and Victoria know how to reverse that process and create loyal customers who will be with you through both the good and bad times.

–Liz Ragland

# Introduction

What is customer service? Have you ever stopped to really think about this question? The literal meaning is serving our customers' needs. But think about that again. Do you really want to be serviced? Or would you rather be wowed? Do you associate happy, grateful, and appreciative with the word "service"? A service is an oil change, not an experience. We removed the phrase "customer service" from our vocabulary a long time ago; we believe that what people really expect is a rewarding experience that keeps them coming back for more. To us, that is customer hospitality.

When you start a business, you soon discover the many different aspects involved. All are important, yet some are overlooked. There are so many responsibilities that must be dealt with every day that it is very difficult to get them all covered. One of the most critical responsibilities you face, and sadly one of the most overlooked, is customer hospitality. Taking care of your customers and exceeding their expectations is a 24-hour-a-day, seven-days-a-week job. Even when your doors are closed, you should still be focused on customer hospitality.

The success of your business involves not just your performance, but also that of every employee. Customer hospitality is more than just meeting people's needs. It is about going above and beyond, making people feel special. Everyone has a bad day now and again, and sometimes associates don't smile or say thank you. *Your Service Sucks* gives you the tools to handle these types of incidents and many more. We'll teach you how to keep your staff motivated and enthusiastic about their jobs, minimize conflict, create an atmosphere of success, and lead your team to greatness.

How well do you and your employees meet the responsibility of providing outstanding customer hospitality? It is critical that each and every customer who comes in contact with your business receives the same high-quality customer hospitality. We've spent more than twenty years working in the customer hospitality field and have seen and heard almost every type of poor customer hospitality out there. We finally had enough and decided to write *Your Service Sucks*. If you're an existing business owner or plan to open a business in the future, a manager of a renegade staff with a bad attitude, or an average Joe on the street fed up with sucky service, this book is for you.

# Chapter 1

Customer Hospitality—Fact or Fiction?

Almost 70 percent of customers who stop doing business with a company do so because they don't receive enough attention, or what they do receive is very poor. What most businesses don't realize is that it takes ten times more money to secure more customers than it does to keep the ones you already have. This statistic was proven by Tom Peters in his book *In Search of Excellence*. As part of the research for his book, he conducted a study to determine why customers leave. His research found the following reasons why customers don't come back:

- **One percent die.**

- **Three percent move.**

- **Five percent give their business to a friend or family.**

- **Nine percent leave because of price.**

- **Fourteen percent leave because of a complaint that wasn't handled correctly or in a timely manner.**

- **Sixty-eight percent leave because they feel they aren't appreciated.**

Even more interesting is that the results of this study haven't changed over the past 20 years. Granted, we don't have much control over the first five points, but it really doesn't matter because they only total 32 percent of your customers. The last point, however, encompasses over half of your business. Wow! That is a lot of customers. The good news is that Your Success Coach can teach you the correct strategies to help you maintain your customers' loyalty and retention.

Do you know why your customers are leaving? Maybe you don't have the right product, or your price is too high. There are numerous reasons people walk out your door, but by far the primary reason your customers leave, vowing never to return, is customer hospitality. At one time or another in our lives, we've all stood in front of a clerk wondering if they recently had a lobotomy. If we were to ask you how many times you've experienced poor customer hospitality, more than likely you could ramble off numerous examples with specific details. But what about good experiences? How many could you recount? One? Two? We can think of countless examples where we experienced poor customer hospitality, but very few that were positive. So, is customer hospitality some elusive creature that lurks in the bushes at night, or does it really exist? Yes, it does exist, and you, your business, and your customers deserve it.

Dale Carnegie said, "You will accomplish more in two months developing a sincere interest in two people than you'll accomplish in the next two years trying to get people interested in you." His words still ring true today—be interested in others and they'll become interested in you. Unlike yesterday, consumers have many options. No longer is the attitude of "take it or leave it" acceptable. The power has shifted from the business owner to the customer. Price no longer is the determining factor for purchases. People want to be treated better and are willing to pay for it. In the past, customers were less apt to voice their opinions about poor hospitality, but that is no longer the case. Today, we are becoming increasingly less tolerant and more demanding of having our expectations not just met but exceeded.

It doesn't matter whether or not your business is a Fortune 500 company or a small street vendor, customer hospitality should be your number one priority. In this day and age of iPhones , Blackberrys, and the Internet, word of mouth is instantaneous, so if one of your employees is rude or disrespectful, it's only a matter of seconds before an email is sent around the world detailing the ordeal and potentially ruining your business in the process. Poor customer hospitality, just like good customer hospitality, will be shared with anyone who listens until the business fails or flourishes. Statistics show that the average dissatisfied customer will tell eight to ten people about their problem. One in five of those will share that with 20 others. So you can see how repeated offenses of poor customer hospitality can quickly snowball into the downfall of *your* business. According to the International Customer Services Association (ICSA), at any one time, 25 percent of your customers are ready to jump ship. All they need is a slight shove to tip them over and then they're gone.

## It's Just One Customer

Answer this one simple question: "Who is the most important person in your business?" If your answer was you or your employees, we're sorry to disappoint you, but that is incorrect. Your customers are the most valuable asset in your business. As a matter of fact, they are your net worth—zero customers, zero net worth! The gift you give to others—how well you serve your customers—determines what you're worth in the future. Lifelong customers provide an endless stream of income. For example, Carl

Sewell's book *Customers for Life* cites a Cadillac salesman in 1990 who claimed on average his clients spent $25,000 per purchase. Over a lifetime people on average purchase 12 cars, so over their lifetime $25,000 x 12 = $300,000. This is the value of a customer for life. Those are 1990 dollars, so just imagine what they would be today! This Potential Lifetime Value, as Carl Sewell called it, demonstrates the value of just one customer.

Leadership expert Ken Blanchard, one of our favorite speakers and authors, has given many lectures and written several books attesting that customers who get upset never say a word; they just walk out the door and vow never to return. They, however, are not shy about telling 10 to twenty other people of their experience. Consider this exponentially (10 tell 10, etc.). Soon, that one customer becomes several thousand. The cost of acquiring new customers is much higher than keeping existing ones. According to the University of Southern California, it costs five to six times more to acquire a new customer than it does to keep your existing ones.

With existing customers, you want to establish and maintain trust by creating a relationship, because you can't create a sale without establishing rapport. Trust is established by you and by the customer, and the outcome is loyalty and retention. Not knowing or caring what's in it for you, but rather worrying about what's in it for them, is a valuable lesson everyone in business should learn. So how do you build that trust? Simple, through the following acronym:

- **V. Visit**
- **I. Invite**
- **P. Present**
- **E. Engage**
- **R. Repeat**

When you build that trust through V.I.P.E.R., everyone within three feet of you are potential customers. Customers will do their absolute *best* to repay you for a lifetime—over and over and over again, which creates loyalty and retention. Because you gave them such good customer hospitality, they become your apostles. An apostle will repay you in kind by bringing you endless referrals. It is important to remember that when you talk to a customer, you're actually talking to four people. "How?" you may be thinking. Simple; everyone has a sphere of influence of at least three people whom they are very close to. So when you are working with customers, keep in mind that they are going to go home and talk to their close friends or family about their customer hospitality experience—*positive or negative.*

Along with this trust, you must learn to master the most underutilized skill out there today—listening. When you listen, you need to hear more than just words. Listening is an active effort; hearing is passive. It's all about reflective or active listening, which is the process of restating, in your own words, the feeling or content that is being expressed by the customer. When you reflect back to customers what you believe you understand, you validate them by giving them the experience of being heard and acknowledged. In addition to validation, you also provide an opportunity for customers to give you feedback.

Customers respond to active listeners. If employees actively listen to their customers, they give the impression that they value what the customer has to say. Managers and other employees spend the majority of their time engaging in passive listening, which causes a misunderstanding of what customers really want. This in turn results in millions of dollars' worth of mistakes just because most employees and managers don't know how to listen. When you're listening, maintain 100 percent eye contact—100 percent. When speaking, break eye contact occasionally. Frame the face. Stay within the frame if you can. Looking too far right or left can cause distractions. Don't think for a minute that the customer won't notice your shift of focus. If you're not interested enough in what they are saying, then why should they buy a product from you? One of the golden rules of customer hospitality is to be there; be present.

Combining trust and listening enables you to activate one of the natural laws of the universe, the Law of Reciprocity. The Law of Reciprocity means that when someone gives you something, you feel an obligation to give back. How many times have you heard the phrase "if you scratch my back, I'll scratch yours"? We need to give and take mutually, and this is definitely true regarding customer hospitality. Customers give back when they've been given to. So when you've given your heart and soul, shown a genuine interest, and tried to help customers with all that you can do, the Law of Reciprocity takes effect, and they will give back to you. Every time you do the right thing for your customers, your employees, your partners, and the community, everyone will try to find a way to repay you with loyalty by giving thoughtful feedback and trying to improve your business. The Law of Reciprocity also means that your customers will tell friends, family, coworkers, and anyone else who will listen to do business with your company. Customer hospitality is about more than sales; it is also about giving unselfishly with an open heart. It's not about *something*— it's about *others*. It's about giving.

Customers have needs beyond the need for your product or service. People have an innate need to feel that they are important and that what they do, think, and say truly matters in this world. You need to make them feel like gold. In that moment, they are all that matters. By failing to actively listen to their needs, you reject them not only as customers but as persons as well. How do you create long-lasting loyalty among your customers? Simple: produce, surprise, delight, and fulfill their needs. Have no expectations of trying to sell to them—customers are already there for a reason; they want to buy but they do not want to be sold to.

Approach customers as if you want to help them, to serve them— all you want to do is help them accomplish their needs. When customers are greeted with sincerity and warmth, by an associate who truly wants to help them, they really don't know how to respond, because they don't experience it often. You have to create a whole new experience. Create miracles for your customers that will be long lasting. Your goal is to get the customer to think "WHOA, what is this?" If you create that customer hospitality miracle, how long do you think the recipient will do business with you? Forever!

## Challenges Businesses Face

There is a good deal of F.E.A.R. (False Evidence Appearing Real) today because of what is going on with the economy and there is no bailout plan for small businesses. If you listen to the news or read the paper, you are endlessly bombarded with doom and gloom. A little nugget of advice for you: turn off the TV, cancel your newspaper, and don't open your investment reports for two years, and concentrate only on taking care of the needs of your customers. Some people, because of the constant negativity, come into your store with a bad attitude. Some are even looking for a fight. This isn't your fault; their behavior is really just a release of anxiety. These feelings of anxiety can occur in associates, too. They're worried about being laid off due to lack of sales, so they seem overanxious and pester the customer. Take a look at the examples below and see if any of them look familiar:

- **A customer walks through the door, already thinking they're not going to get what they want. They're influenced by conditions outside of their lives and expecting the worst, so they are constantly on guard.**

- **The associate has a fear that they're not going to make the sale.**

- **The business owner is thinking, "Oh my God, I'm not going to make enough money to even make payroll."**

Small businesses employ more people than any other industry, and they're going out of business left and right. Meeting the needs of your customers is the single most important aspect of business, and those businesses that manage to do this effectively, invariably have more customers, retain them, and ultimately make more money. More often than not, employees ignore dissatisfied customers or don't have enough knowledge to answer questions about products or services. All too often, we see where an employee makes a choice to ignore dissatisfied customers with the hope that they will just go away. They choose not to engage in the conflict or pass it off to someone else. The employee mistakenly thinks, "Oh well, what is the loss of one customer?" The problem is, it is not just one customer. Remember the sphere of three people that everyone has?

Some of the challenges businesses face today include the following:

- **Poorly designed systems and procedures. The employees don't know the why behind the system or procedures, or why they are needed, or what the value of them is. The main reason for this is because the employees weren't involved in designing the systems and procedures.**

- **Lack of empowerment. Employees are not empowered to make decisions. If they were, they could make them quickly to help salvage the customer and the situation. They are often told to recite policies and *that's it*. They have to say, "Our store policy is X, Y, Z ..." instead of being allowed to think creatively to make the customer happy. The ideal situation would be to allow them to break the rules but know where the boundaries are. Boundaries** need to be flexible like a rubber band (able to bend but not break).

- Modeling. Monkey see, monkey do. If employees see their supervisor breaking the rules or offering poor customer hospitality, then it is only natural that they will do the same. The bosses, even in upper management, all aren't doing it—they're not creating the right behavior to model after. We have to set a good example for our employees. Also, if management isn't providing feedback, then how can employees know if they are doing the job incorrectly? The associates aren't given any reason as to why; they have no information—they only have the slice of bread, not the whole loaf.

- Training. In most cases, companies don't have, or aren't willing to spend the money on training. Oftentimes, they spend money in the wrong places, such as product development. This is good in theory, but if you don't have any customers, who are you going to sell your products to? Training is where their greatest investment should be. Service people who face challenges without training— who go head-to-head with the customer—don't know what to do and 99 percent of the time, lose that customer.

- Continual turnover. The frontline positions are the ones that face continual turnover because these people are typically not trained to be effective in their respective positions. They are placed on the floor and told, "OK, here are the keys; go for it." Also, these frontline associates are many times slashed and burned by customers, management, and each other. As a result, they quit or get fired. Management doesn't care; these positions are easy to fill, so their thought process is "Next!" They just find another employee to replace the one who left. Associate after associate, there is a constant turnover because of the lack of training. We need to set them up to succeed instead of setting them up to fail in their positions.

Behavior begets behavior. How you behave determines your outcome. When negativity is allowed to enter, it festers and spreads like a disease. Don't treat customer hospitality as a chore. It actually can take more energy emotionally to deliver average or poor hospitality than excellent hospitality. Why is that so? Because when you show you care for your customers, you're building relationships, thus ensuring repeat business and making your job easier. In addition, you feel better about yourself when you deliver superb customer hospitality—don't you? It's more satisfying. People will jump at the opportunity to be served well because it's so rare.

## Go the Extra Mile

Customers are shocked when they receive exceptional customer hospitality because they are used to being treated so badly. The standard seems to be so low in most businesses, or at least that is how it appears to most customers. The businesses that will survive this economic crisis are the ones that excel in customer hospitality. Going above and beyond to really understand what your customers want and need is critical to the survival of businesses today and for the next several years.

Small gestures, like a smile and a friendly hello, can go further than you know. We recently went on a golfing trip to Arizona and were paying close attention to the different levels of customer hospitality we received. We must admit that we even expect poor customer hospitality as a standard. When we received exceptional customer hospitality, we were so pleased that we wrote down most of our experiences. We also wrote down the bad ones. There is a *huge* difference in the levels you receive. It seems to be either really, really bad or superb. There really isn't much in between.

Here's an example. We pulled up to a golf course at a resort called the Phoenician. It had a guard station, and a gentleman appeared from the door with a smile and asked us why we were visiting. We explained that we were there to play golf and he said, "Well, today they're swinging the canes over to your right." He pointed us on our way and wished us well. He was pleasant and funny, and we spoke for no more than ten seconds, yet he left us feeling welcomed and warm. One of the people with us even commented, "You see! If people would just take a second to make people feel welcome—it makes all the difference in the world!"

An example of the type of hospitality we are used to is what we experienced while renting a car. The gentleman in front of us had almost finished his transaction and requested a GPS unit. You would have thought he asked to cop a feel the way the girl behind the counter acted. At the speed of a snail, she slid out of her chair and shuffled her feet as if she were on a death march to retrieve the unit. After what seemed like twelve hours and thirty minutes, she finally emerged from the back, chunked the GPS on the counter, and sat back down. Her actions could have been the result of two scenarios. One, her legs suffered from some genetic disorder that required her to immediately sit down after only a few moments of movement; or two, she was just the laziest person on earth who had absolutely no customer hospitality training. We're guessing it was the latter of the two.

She took her time and brought it to him in a bag and just handed it to him—as if the transaction was complete. No "Thank you" or "Can I help you?" Nothing. Just like George on *Seinfeld*, "He got nothing." The customer had no idea how to use the GPS, so he said very politely, "I've never used one of these before; can you give me some instruction?" She hesitantly gave him the briefest lesson she could muster. To this day, we wonder if this guy isn't lying on the side of a dirt road somewhere still trying to figure how to work the GPS. While we were waiting to be helped, there was a gentleman behind the counter reading a romance novel. The other associate asked for assistance so we could be helped and without even looking up, he said, "I'm not on the clock." And that was that! With customer hospitality like this, we can't imagine why there could possibly be a lack of confidence from the customer.

One of the reasons for the lack of customer hospitality is that associates oftentimes don't know what their jobs are, but they also don't know how to ask questions. As business owners and managers, we need to teach our employees how to use leading questions with "what" and "how" to meet the customer's needs. Find out what the true needs are and dig deep. "What" and "how" at the beginning of questions helps to create personal responsibility; see, for example, questions such as "What can I do for you today?" "How can I help you?" and "What is it I can do?" Create reasons why they need your product or services. You see, the "whys" and "hows" create movement and action.

There are policies all over the company, and no one understands that customers are, or should be, behind every policy. They don't understand the "what" and the "how" they contribute to the organization. Associates often don't know what their piece of the puzzle is—they've never been shown that. Management never asks the associates what their dreams are, what they want out of life, and what they want for their personal lives; therefore they work for "the man," never seeing the bigger picture.

Management has got to ask their associates what they want to accomplish out of their life and then tie it into their current job. Doing so creates an atmosphere where management and associates are working for the same common goal. Your organization has to take an interest in associates. For instance, let's say an employee wants to buy a home. Management could help the employee by explaining, "If you make two extra sales a day, you get more commissions, which puts you one step closer to your new home." This is a win-win situation. Not only have you helped your employee accomplish a goal, but you've also gotten more sales. Take an interest in your staff and ask what they want, and you can help them to achieve it. If the company would tie what the employees' goals are in line with what the organization's goals are, showing that they care about their people, they would achieve far better results. If you give associates what they want, they will give you what you want: quid pro quo. As a result, customers will then get what they want.

The more you grow in customer hospitality awareness, the better you understand customers' needs and what makes them continue to walk through your door. This understanding gives you the opportunity and knowledge to create repeat business and increase your profit. With this knowledge, you can start to make conscious decisions to train your employees and increase customer satisfaction. If you don't actively make this decision as an owner or operator, your associates will stay in the same old habits as before, and no change for the better can take place. This causes many unnecessary headaches for you and fosters chaos in your company. Stop for a moment and think about the correlation between your associates' actions and your results. We've created the Levels of Mastery to help you determine where your staff is in relation to customer hospitality. They are as follows:

- **Ignorance. This is the stage where most businesses are today. The customer is not considered an asset and treated as such.**

- **Awareness. This is when your employees have transactional interactions with clients. They act in an almost robotic manner, just going through the motions repeating company phrases or policies, not fully understanding the meaning behind them.**

- **Motivation.** At this stage, your staff is able to perform a minimum amount of customer hospitality when under supervision. Customer hospitality is a "have to" mindset rather than a "want to" mindset.

- **Structural.** Once the associates enter this level, they are able to retain a certain amount of training and then relay that in their interactions with the customers with a maximum amount of confidence.

- **Commitment.** Once associates hit this stage, they are fully committed not only to your product or service but to you also.

- **Retention.** Your associates are fully engaged. They want to see the company succeed and will do whatever it takes to make it happen. They are happy, and their needs are being met by you and management, so they stop looking elsewhere for employment. They feel like they've found a home.

- **Loyalty.** This is the highest Level of Mastery. At this stage, your employees have the knowledge and desire to exceed the needs of their customers. They are empowered to make decisions based on what they believe to be to the best benefit of the client.

## C.A.R.E.: Concern, Appreciate, Respect, Empathize

Oftentimes, associates don't even know the company's mission statement or the meaning behind it. They don't know their value, and they don't know what they contribute to the company and what their role in the company is. Management may give them a slice of bread, but won't give them the whole loaf! They don't know where they fit in.

Forum Corporation conducted a study to define and measure successful practices in customer hospitality. In their research, they found that

- **15 percent left because they found a better product.**

- **15 percent left because they found a cheaper product.**

- **20 percent left because there was too little contact or personal attention.**

- **50 percent left because the hospitality they had received was poor in quality (indifference—who cares?).**

Associates need to become artfully skilled in being able to identify body language, tone, and mannerisms. The way customers say things and how they say things are all important elements in reading a situation. That goes for associates as well. When associates are dealing with customers, they read your body language also, yet these people never tell you what they are thinking at the time. This *silent majority* can cost your business the most. In fact, 96 percent of the silent majority—unless you pick up on their cues—will be gone forever. The second they walk out the door, they're telling everybody about their bad experience and they'll never come back and the associate and possibly management has *no clue* that they did anything wrong. They didn't care enough to notice that the customer reacted to something they've said. C.A.R.E. enough to notice!

It is imperative that management train and empower associates to make decisions to take care of their customers. A good method of doing this is to include them in decisions that affect them and to teach them to make their own decisions. Even if they make the wrong decision, let them know that it's okay and that it can be corrected and used as a learning tool. Working with your staff in this manner helps them to grow in self-confidence and self-esteem as well as helps them to take personal responsibility and accountability for their actions.

The role of customer hospitality in a business is essential for its growth and survival, and it depends on the quality of hospitality you deliver. Customers grade you every day by how much they spend. If your competitor is getting a better grade, they are making more money than *you*. If organizations fail to recognize this, they will wither and die. The success of your business is dependent on the way you treat and interact with your customers. No customers, no money, no jobs, no business.

Your customers are your company's most valuable asset and advertising tool. They will offer your business an advertising tool that is beyond words—word-of-mouth advertising. You're creating those apostles we discussed earlier. This will only happen, however, if your customers are happy and have their expectations exceeded. Remember, a miracle creates an apostle. An apostle is the greatest sales force you'll ever have. In addition to advertising your business, they'll increase the chances of getting repeat business from happy and satisfied customers.

Without customer hospitality, a business will not be able to survive or sustain itself. Exceeding customers' expectations should be the foremost principle of your company. You must work toward building a relationship with your customers where they provide you feedback for future growth and improvement of your business. Remember, the cost of exceptional hospitality is zero, yet the potential return is millions of dollars.

## Advantages of Customer Hospitality and Focusing on Customer Hospitality

- You focus on promoting the success of others.

- It builds self-gratification immensely for the associates.

- It builds self-confidence in associates and consumers.

- Focusing on the success of others and making sure their needs have been met guarantees that yours will be met and fulfilled. It also guarantees that loyalty and commitment will come in some form or fashion.

- Your business's reputation grows and improves.

- Giving a feeling of significance to everyone you come in contact with is vitally important.

- Customers want to feel listened to and heard so you can help them get what they need to get. Help them have what they need to have.

- Customers want to feel significant, and if you act in a way that shows you care about the community, your reputation will grow as a result.

- You are making them feel significant by allowing them to be who they are.

- There is added value that you are even there, making them feel significant.

- The customer then becomes your best advertising.

- Your company and name are being talked about out in the world in a positive manner.

- One-on-one personal referrals are the best advertising.

- You forge a bond that consumers share with everyone they know—a bond of trust is formed in their sphere of influence where they go out and say, "You know what? They just took care of me." They're saying something else about you other than negativity.

- There is a distinction between you and your competition that cannot be replaced!

- You achieve customer loyalty.

# Action Steps

1. Create a mission statement or a purpose statement.

2. Create your business or personal value statement.

3. Write out the top six things you do daily to serve your purpose and mission.

4. What training and advance learning can you pursue to help you achieve your mission and purpose?

5. What is the "why" behind your policies and procedures you work with and how do these affect you and your customers?

# Chapter 2

## What Do You Mean My Service Sucks?

What do you mean my service sucks? Just asking if a person needs help or pointing them in the direction of the product they're looking for isn't customer hospitality. Vanna White may be able to make a living gracefully waving her hands and smiling, but you need to do much more than that. In fact, this type of hospitality sucks not only for your customers but for *you* as well because you probably just lost a potential client to your competition. These economic times are tough, and whether you want to believe it or not, *you* are privileged to have a person walk into your establishment, not the other way around. So take a look at your employees and the next time you see Drusilla dressed in black velvet sporting her latest tongue piercing while twisting her hair and rolling her eyes as *your* customers walk out the door, think about how Drusilla affects your bottom line.

Some reasons for poor customer hospitality include the following:

- **A general lack of personal responsibility and accountability by the employee if a customer leaves angry. This includes everyone from upper management to frontline associates.**

- An attitude of coloring within the lines and staying within the box. When employees have this type of attitude, they will not take the initiative. They will not *think*. Employees starting out with a transaction will not be flexible or caring when a customer has an issue. Instead, they'll recite policies and procedures, and create barriers that are (in their minds) written in stone and will thereby not take care of the customer's needs.

- Not listening and not caring about customers' needs. This leads to miscommunication, malfunction, and chaos. The tone is one of interrogation, not concern. The response is "Whatever" instead of "We'll be happy to take care of it." And the result is never exactly what the customer wanted.

- Modeling performance and behavior from leadership and management. More often than not, management sets a bad example by avoiding customers, not paying attention to them, or making themselves inaccessible to customers. This type of behavior sets the standard for employees. They mirror management's actions and the tendency becomes "Do as I do, not as I say."

- Management not monitoring behavior of frontline associates. Allowing employees to say "no" to a customer does not solve their problem, resulting in them leaving your establishment angry.

- Leadership and management not monitoring and measuring the performance and behavior of frontline associates. If your frontline associates don't know they are acting incorrectly due to lack of feedback and lack of training, then they don't know what else to do. For example, allowing the employee to say "no" to a customer should be forbidden. Teaching them to say "Here is what we can do" instead of "no" is vital. "No" never solves the customer's issue; it just makes them angry. When this happens, you have a very small window to resolve the issues.

- **Lack of money spent on the training budget.** One of the major Fortune 400 companies in the world decided to almost entirely eliminate their training development. As a result, it experienced drastic declines in revenue due to poorly trained associates. If your company not only promotes customer hospitality, but goes even deeper to provide other personal development training, this shows the associates that you care about them as people and then they will work harder for you. Current large corporate training benchmarks show that only minimal acceptable standards are being met.

Many times, we don't realize the importance of perception. What we perceive to be true isn't always the case. For instance, the 75-year-old grandpa in a Speedo swimsuit may think he looks good, but to everyone else, he's just ruined their lunch. A person's perception is actually the most important aspect of any situation. In business, particularly customer hospitality, perception *is* reality. You can think you're doing the best job in the world, but if your customers don't believe so, then that's all that matters. When a company is delivering superior customer hospitality, perception by the customer is very different than that of an associate. You have to be able to actively listen and understand what your customers are sharing through words, tone, and body language in order to discern their needs.

We've all heard the phrase "Perception is in the eye of the beholder" and this is certainly the case with your customers. Businesses are struggling all across the country, not so much because of the economy, but more because of the public's poor perception of their service, behavior, and performance. This doesn't have to be the case; we must increase our awareness about our public image and constantly improve upon it. It is unrealistic to think that we're "good enough." There is always room for improvement. Mediocrity and the status quo don't cut it anymore. You have to stay several steps ahead of your competitors.

The title of this book—*Your Service Sucks. And Your Competition Loves You for It!*—may or may not be true in some cases. But if your service does suck, we guarantee you that your competition does love you for it. They're like vultures swirling overhead, just waiting for the slightest mistake so they can swoop down and steal your customers. That particular customer you've just lost because an associate says "It's our policy ..." or "Sorry, there is no one here presently who can help with this issue," or through any other boneheaded mistakes like not being friendly, showing absolutely no interest in the customer as a person, or overpromising and way underdelivering, will delight your competition because your customer has just gone to them. You only get one chance to make a first impression, and the one you and your staff make is forever ingrained in the public's mind. (We'll discuss more on first impressions in chapter five.)

### Wrinkle-Resistant Shirt—50 Dollars, Money Saved on Starch—20 Dollars, Customer Hospitality—Priceless

Here's an eye-opener —most customers are treated badly. Do you realize that only eight percent of customers believe that companies provide excellent customer hospitality? Most customers' expectations are never matched and they feel that the attitudes of the associates are horrible. The economic times are making people crazy, fearful, and stressed. They're insecure about the future. Lots of people have lost their jobs, and the stock market has plummeted. While these issues reflect the global economy, they aren't your primary focus. Your primary focus should be your customers, because without them, you don't have a business.

When we were writing this section, the movie *Pretty Woman* came to mind. When Richard Gere tossed Julia Roberts a handful of credit cards and told her to ditch the "ho" attire, she streetwalked (sorry we couldn't resist) up and down Rodeo Drive and no one would give her the time of day, until the two of them went together and Richard offered an "obscene amount" of money in return for a healthy dose of "sucking up." Remember at the end of the scene, when Julia went back to one of the boutiques, asked if they worked on commission and when they said yes, held up her bags and said, "Big mistake"? This is a classic example of how perception can and will cost you money.

We need to go a step further and discuss not only the virtues of customer hospitality but also customer loyalty and retention. There is a huge difference between a satisfied customer and a loyal customer. As Jeffery Gitomer points out in his book *Customer Satisfaction is Worthless. Customer Loyalty is Priceless,* the contrast lies in the fact that satisfied customers may and often do shop anywhere, whereas loyal customers will fight to stay with you and bring as many of their friends along with them as they can. Your loyal customers and their referrals—your W.O.M.M. team (word-of-mouth marketing = W.O.M.M)—becomes your most powerful marketing tool.

Here's a learned skill we want to provide you with so you can increase your awareness and learn to be more sensitive to the customer's internal and external perceptions. A quick note: this is not a onetime lesson; you have to strive to maintain a constant state of awareness and sensitivity. Listen closely to what is really being said to you and also to what's not being said. Become a solution provider, not a problem maker. Paying more attention to customer perception will supercharge your customer hospitality reputation, your subsequent sales figures, and your profits$$$$. The International Customer Service Association (ICSA) statistics show that a company that provides exceptional customer hospitality averages about 32 percent more profit than a company that provides mediocre hospitality. Excellent customer hospitality has a direct correlation to a higher profit margin.

A benefit of excellent customer hospitality is customer loyalty. This, too, is essential to the success of your business. You can't always rely on someone new to walk through your doors every day, but you can rely on the same stream of people who know you and your service to help you through both the good and bad times. Price has no bearing on purchase decision. Where would you rather shop: a retail outlet with loud music blaring and the prom king and queen standing behind the counter watching the clock? Or an outlet with a responsible associate who is willing to stay late and answer any questions you may have?

No matter who you believe to be the most important person in the world, customers want to feel that *they* are number one. When a customer calls with an issue, do you say anything like these quotes?

- "It's our policy."

- "Hold on." (That one really pisses us off.)

- "I'd like to help you with this, but the person you need to speak with is not in today."

- "We're very busy right now. May I call you back?'

- "It's not my job."

- "Sorry, I can't help you. Our policy states that all sales are final."

When you give answers like the ones above, or worse, your customers get an answering machine, you're not displaying customer hospitality or anything of the kind. You really aren't helping at all. Just one of those statements used one time can lose you this customer and many more. Our point here is that your customers are frustrated and if they aren't treated with the *best* customer hospitality ever, you aren't going to see them again. Who pays you? Provides money for your paycheck? If you answered your boss or the company, we're sorry to tell you that you're wrong. It's the customer who pays you.

So exactly just how do you acquire a loyal customer base? First, you need to realize that all of your customers aren't going to maintain the same level of loyalty. One may visit every week and spend a small amount while another may only call on you twice a year, yet spend a large sum of money with you each time. Both of these scenarios are okay; all that matters is that the customers keep coming back.

Another aspect of loyalty is your unique service or product as well as the customer hospitality they experience. As we mentioned earlier, people expect the best but settle for mediocre, so when you go above and beyond exceeding their expectations, you create repeat business and valuable positive word-of-mouth advertising. If you want to develop customer loyalty, you have to understand where the loyalties of your existing customers lie and accommodate them accordingly. When your business manages and maintains customer loyalty, your business will increase exponentially and each new customer soon becomes a long-standing one.

## I Don't Get Paid to Do That ...

Have you ever experienced a situation in which the person waiting on you gets mad at you because they made a poor career choice? Unfortunately, there are people in customer hospitality who have huge chips on their shoulders. We've experienced this numerous times. One time in particular stands out in our minds. A friend of ours said that during the spring and summer, they have a young man who mows their yard each week. One Friday evening, he rang their doorbell to collect on his bill (why he didn't mail it is still a mystery) and when one of them told the other that the "yard guy" is at the front door, he became agitated and said, "Hey, I'm not the yard guy, I'm a landscape engineer." Okay, whatever you say, but the reality is that you're a guy who mows their yard. Needless to say, they no longer use him. The fact that you aren't happy in your present position doesn't give you any right to treat your customers badly.

Another favorite is the young person standing behind the counter glaring at you because they feel a sense of entitlement and believe that they shouldn't be working. Disclaimer time: by no means are we stating or making a claim that all young people have poor work ethics. We just notice a saddening trend in our society. Take it from us, everyone should work one or two grunt jobs to appreciate the good ones. An honest job is a good job, and it doesn't matter what type of work you do; you should do it to your best ability with the realization that your actions affect others.

When you hear remarks such as "That's not my job," "I'm not paid to do that," or "It's not my responsibility" you need to remind your associates that anytime they have *any type* of interaction with a customer, it *is* their job because the customers pay their salaries. From their perspective, they are doing the job they are paid for and don't realize the potential impact of offending customers. Both managers and associates need take note of how they act and communicate with customers as well as pay attention to what customers want. Some of these include

- **Not to be left on hold when calling.**

- **The ability to speak to a live person rather than listen to an endless automated phone service.**

- **To be treated like they are the most important person on the planet.**

- To feel you care about their needs.

- To feel that you are truly listening.

- Not to be treated like "next" customer.

- Create a magical environment with clear dialogue and a caring and concerned attitude to accommodate their needs, and even exceed their needs. To keep your customers loyal you need to:

- Start with yes—get to the solution by whatever means necessary.

- Be memorable.

- Surprise customers and be genuinely interested.

- Underpromise and overdeliver.

- Go above and beyond and create an eager *want.*

- Smile and treat them as if they are your only customer and talk in terms of their interest.

- Make them feel special by actively listening to their needs. Remember, listening is the sincerest form of flattery.

- Enhance relationships.

- Become a friendly person.

- Give honest and sincere appreciation.

- Remember their name; a customer's name is the sweetest and most important sound they like to hear.

- Last but not least, ask your customer for help *and* ask them for feedback.

Just as in all aspects of life, there are positive people and there are negative people. Recognizing those who create a poor perception for your customers is critical. When you notice a problem such as this with your associates, it is important to take action, whether it is to send them to training, coach them, or mentor them yourself. Creating a good customer perception is a continuous process, and on occasion, even the best associates can regress. Benchmark performance sets the standard and demands that it be met. Monitor, measure, and follow up. Here's a good process to keep in mind: tell me, show me, watch me do, and evaluate me. A counterpart to that is continuous improvement. W. Edwards Deming promoted this concept effectively through the Deming Wheel, which utilizes the Plan, Do, Check, and Act approach to continuous improvement as follows:

- **Plan. Identify the issue and its root causes.**

- **Do. Select, develop, and implement a solution for the issue.**

- **Check. Evaluate the results. Did it achieve your desired goal?**

- **Act. Identify the necessary changes and training needs to adopt and implement the solution. Continue to look additional improvement opportunities to refine the solution.**

Remember, there is no such thing as perfect, but you can work toward continuous improvement. The Deming Wheel helps you to coordinate your continuous improvement efforts by emphasizing and demonstrating that improvement programs must start with careful planning, result in effective action, and move forward to careful planning in a continuous cycle. In any field, especially customer hospitality, we must strive for continuous improvement. This is the only way we can move forward and hone in on our expertise.

## Feedback, Feedback, and More Feedback

Personality can have a lot to do with how we treat people in daily life and in work. For instance, you make your numbers, and may even have a few loyal customers, but that doesn't mean you're giving exceptional customer hospitality. The goal every day should be to treat everyone the way you treat your very best customer. This may be difficult due to the personalities that come your way. The ability to interpret and respond to different social styles is critical. You must have the awareness of these styles and have the ability to adapt your behavior to theirs and make them more comfortable. Doing so provides you with a more successful business. There are many methods for determining social styles, which will be discussed in depth later in this text.

You have the ability to create a loyal customer or an angry consumer who calls the local news hotline. You have to listen to what they mean, not what they're saying, as well as know how they feel when they walk out the door. What distinguishes one company from another in today's competitive marketplace is their ability to provide exceptional customer hospitality. It is our responsibility to ensure that customers have a positive and memorable experience. When a person makes a decision to shop with you or acquire your services, you have to let them know you care about them and value their business.

Complaints are inevitable in any business. The world we live in is not perfect, so it is imperative to handle a disgruntled customer correctly. In doing so, you can transform what was once seemingly a monster ready to devour Tokyo into a sweet little old lady who will tell her entire bridge group about how fabulous you are. The method with which you deal with the initial contact of an angry customer should not be to run and hide underneath your desk or "accidentally" hang up on them. Instead, defuse the situation in a manner that isn't adversarial or accusatory. You may be right and that size three pair of jeans they are returning didn't fit them before they were washed in hot water, but you're still representing your company and that single pair of size three jeans can potentially turn into several sales later down the line when their diet pays off.

Don't take these disagreements personally. They aren't mad at you; they are mad at the circumstance or issue that needs to be resolved. Refrain from becoming defensive and take control of the situation. Listen attentively and show them respect. You have to be diplomatic in your actions and words. Yes, you may want to jump over the counter and strangle them, but since that is obviously not an option, smile, *breathe,* and remain calm. If you can do this for your difficult customers, think about how well you will be able to treat your best customers.

Is the customer who gives you a hard time wrong? Are you doing such a stupendous job that people would consider you perfect? Most conflicts need to be responded to in different ways to provide a variety of solutions. In the world of customer hospitality, there is no right or wrong. The objective is not to win, but to make the customer happy. Handling difficult customers can be challenging, yes, but it is well worth mastering the negotiation skills required to win their loyalty. Remember, your customers are your lifeline, so the happier they are, the more successful you are.

The perception about your business should never be overlooked. Evaluate and get feedback from your customers and associates on a regular basis to help you determine if their expectations are being met and exceeded by you and your company. Unless you have experienced either exceptional customer hospitality or horrible customer hospitality, you may not be aware of how you treat people.

So how do you know what kind of hospitality you're giving? To gauge customers' satisfaction, giving them a questionnaire similar to everyone else is pointless. The real judge is to ask your customer to describe the most memorable event that happened during their last transaction with you. There are many ways of doing this, depending on the type of business you're in. Some of these questions can include the following:

- **Share with us your most memorable experience while shopping in our store.**

- **Share your experience with any associate you encountered. How did they meet or exceed your needs? Describe in as much detail as possible.**

- **Describe a memorable event that you will tell others about.**

- **Describe a positive or negative experience when calling the business.**

This exercise gives us the feedback we must have in order to take appropriate action and reward exceptional behavior or get more training, coaching, and mentoring to those who give mediocre or poor hospitality. The goal always needs to be to create loyal customers, not just satisfied ones. Mediocrity is easy. Being exceptional takes effort and a desire to be the best. Every day, we have experiences with customers, and as a result of these interactions, they leave with their own perception of us and our business. We may think we know them and what they want, but in reality we actually know very little. We often forget that we are only as good as our customers' perception of us. We are only as good as our associates' perceptions of us. How we are perceived determines our prosperity. Whether we like it or not, we can't gauge the success of our business from our own perception. Perception is 100 percent of reality; it is definitely in the eye of the beholder.

# Action Steps

1. Ask your staff if they know the difference between listening and active listening.

2. Write down what you think the perception of your business is and then take a survey among your customers. Was it the same?

3. Take the following statements and write an alternate, positive response beside each one.

- "It's our policy."

- "Hold on."

- "I'd like to help you with this, but the person you need to speak with is not in today."

- "Were very busy right now. May I call you back?'

- "It's not my job."

- "Sorry, I can't help you. Our policy states that all sales are final."

# Chapter 3

## Different Strokes for Different Folks

Over 75 percent of our success in business stems from our ability to connect with people and engender rapport, establish credibility, and build trust. This is especially true in the marketplace today. Your name tag may say "Sales Associate," but you are much more than that. You're a customer yourself. The "Golden Rule" proposes treating customers the way *you* want to be treated. The "Platinum Rule" says treat them the way *they* want to be treated. Perhaps it's time for a new rule taking the high road of empathic listening, the "Diamond Rule™": *Treat the customer as if they are the most important customer who has ever walked through your door.* Part of the Diamond Rule™ is to create moments of truth when the encounter occurs between the employee and the customer. For that brief moment that customer feels like they are the most important person in the world. There are *zero defects* in building a great relationship when you:

- Take the initiative to learn all about the customer in front of you.

- Remain positive and engaging, and reflect back their needs.

- Make sure you make the customer feel visible, not invisible.

- Are warm and compassionate, not cold and impersonal.

Given the information about the Diamond Rule™ above, with all the talents you have as an exceptional hospitality provider, you will come across many different personality traits and behavioral styles that will differ from your own. Your ability to adapt to these different styles gives you a competitive advantage. Regarding these different traits and styles, perception is 100 percent of their reality. It will rarely be the same as yours. The skill you need is your ability to master the adaptation process in order to build a relationship, retention, and loyalty.

There are times when you are a detective, educator, cheerleader, coach, leader, influencer, and perhaps the occasional punching bag. You always have to be an exceptional listener, however. Having a pleasing personality is one of the most important characteristics of providing exceptional hospitality, and it just starts with a smile and has an element of creativity. Having the hospitality attitude, where the needs of the client come before your own, is essential.

No matter which facet of the public you work with, educating them is always going to be part of the process. In part, your job is to help your customer decide what they need to be happy with your product or service. So here's a crash course in behaviors for you to incorporate and commit to doing all the time, not 90 percent, not 95 percent, but 100 percent of the time:

- **Always listen more than you talk.**

- **Always allow people to finish their sentences.**

- **Always accept and consider other people's ideas; never disregard them.**

- **Always maintain the importance of their creativity and imagination in their ability to share it with others.**

- **Always say "Please" and "Thank you" when speaking to others.**

You must be able to adapt and allow yourself to look beyond the current situation and view it from your customer's eyes. Looking through their eyes helps you to better understand the opportunities you have to help them and to strengthen the relationship by acknowledging and adapting to their behaviors. It's easy if you think about customer hospitality rule number one—The customer is always right! (coined by Philadelphia retailer John Wanamaker) And if you forget rule number one, go to rule number two—there is no rule number two!

REMEMBER ME? "I'm the fellow who goes into a restaurant, sits down and patiently waits while the waitresses do everything but take my order. I'm the fellow who goes into a department store and stands quietly while the sales clerks finish their little chitchat. I'm the man who drives into a gasoline station and never blows his horn, but waits patiently while the attendant finishes reading his comic book. Yes, you might say I'm a good guy. But you know who else I am? I am the Fellow Who Never Comes Back, and it amuses me to see you spending thousands of dollars every year to get me back into your store, when I was there in the first place, and all you had to do to keep me was Give Me a Little Hospitality; Show Me a Little Courtesy." *Anonymous* (We ought to all have name tags and always smile).

## Self-Test on Your Pleasing Personality

On a scale of 1 to 5 rate these behaviors
(1 being lowest, 5 being the highest):

| | | | | | |
|---|---|---|---|---|---|
| Positive mental attitude | 1 | 2 | 3 | 4 | 5 |
| Using a pleasing tone of voice | 1 | 2 | 3 | 4 | 5 |
| Alertness of mind | 1 | 2 | 3 | 4 | 5 |
| Willingness to listen | 1 | 2 | 3 | 4 | 5 |
| Flexibility and adaptation | 1 | 2 | 3 | 4 | 5 |
| Patience | 1 | 2 | 3 | 4 | 5 |
| Timing of your words | 1 | 2 | 3 | 4 | 5 |
| Being open-minded | 1 | 2 | 3 | 4 | 5 |
| Looking for opportunities | 1 | 2 | 3 | 4 | 5 |
| Looking at limitations | 1 | 2 | 3 | 4 | 5 |
| Tactfulness of speech | 1 | 2 | 3 | 4 | 5 |
| Proper manners | 1 | 2 | 3 | 4 | 5 |
| Consideration | 1 | 2 | 3 | 4 | 5 |
| Promptness | 1 | 2 | 3 | 4 | 5 |
| Procrastination | 1 | 2 | 3 | 4 | 5 |
| Thinking of others before yourself | 1 | 2 | 3 | 4 | 5 |
| Physical appearance | 1 | 2 | 3 | 4 | 5 |
| Being dramatic and inspiring | 1 | 2 | 3 | 4 | 5 |
| Celebrating life's little victories | 1 | 2 | 3 | 4 | 5 |
| Honesty | 1 | 2 | 3 | 4 | 5 |
| Trustworthiness | 1 | 2 | 3 | 4 | 5 |

Total Score: _____

How'd you do? Add up your score.

81 and higher: You're a Rockin' Hospitality Agent.

60–80: You're headed in the right direction to becoming a customer hospitality expert.

Below 60: You may want to rethink your profession (Never be the reason the customer doesn't come back!).

Will Rogers said, *"People learn more from observation than conversation."*

According to the Strategic Planning Institute, "Companies that are rated high in customer service gain market share faster, have higher return on sales, have double profit margins, and charge more for their products and services." Let us give you an example: In 1993, Domino's Pizza changed their service guarantee from "30 minutes or $3 off" to "Total Satisfaction or Your Money Back!" That was in 1993—we're in 2009. Where do you think it takes us NOW?

It pertains to people skills and customer hospitality; you want to project a professional image that encourages mutual respect. Their time is valuable, but so is yours. Know your customers' buying motives. Make it easy for people to buy from you. People love to "buy" but they hate to be "sold." Your customers don't care how much you know... until they know how much you care about them and what their needs are. Your main goal here is to interact with customers, let them get to know you, and ultimately develop a relationship. Always do more than is expected. Always be courteous and polite. Remember, the customer is our reason for being here. The key is to maintain the relationship and make your customer feel valued. Here are two good examples of what not to do:

- **Tell an upset customer to grow up and get a life.**

- **Hang up on the company's biggest customer three times.**

The voice of the customer must be heard. Feedback is vital for the relationship to develop and grow. From the feedback we get from customers, we provide better hospitality. We walk the talk. And when we're seen walking the talk, the consistency creates credibility. Clients appreciate it, and in return, we get loyalty and retention.

## You Say "Neither" and I Say "Nyther"

Not every customer is going to have the same personality or act in the same way. This can be a challenge. Monday, you may work with three of the nicest people in the world, and on Friday, you meet this spawn of Satan. That's the majority of any business. You have to be prepared. Because of these differences, both you and your staff need to understand the different types of customers in the marketplace today.

Each one of us is unique in our own way. No two people are exactly the same. We all display different characteristics, especially when confronted with the reality of making a large purchase or having to talk to a stranger about a product we need. For some, the gift of gab enables them to talk to a salesperson with ease. Others just see an associate, look to the ground, turn away, or in some cases, stick their head in the display case like an ostrich hiding in the sand.

Accepting and understanding the fact that customers are different, and therefore need to be treated as such, is integral to the success of your business. Whether you are a small business owner, manager, or employee, the key to creating a loyal customer base depends on your ability to identify the differences in people and cater to their specific needs. As a customer hospitality representative, you need to be able to identify many different behavioral styles and then find a way to communicate with them. A timid man who isn't really sure what he wants won't respond to an in-your-face sales approach. In the same manner, an outgoing vibrant personality won't connect with a clerk who mumbles and stands behind the counter like his feet are in a bucket of cement.

When you learn to deal appropriately with the different customer types, you'll soon find it much easier to establish trust, credibility, and rapport with them. Another great benefit of this is that you'll see an increase in sales too. One important point to remember is that loyal customers make up only 20 percent of your business, and account for over half of your sales. So, if you have a stark-raving lunatic who rides the kiddy merry-go-round outside your door while eating candy corn, remember they are a loyal paying customer, and you have to learn to deal with their eccentricities.

If you intend on developing your business and increasing revenue, you must focus on customer hospitality. Rule number one—don't judge your customers. The fact that they're buying handcuffs, a dog collar, and a Kenny G CD shouldn't taint your opinion of them. Everyone has a different background and belief system. By finding the differences, you can gain valuable information to help you better work with your client. Find out their perspectives during your initial greeting by letting them tell you what they are looking for and asking questions. Once you gain an understanding of their wants and needs, you can find out what is truly important to them.

Keep in mind that you have hired rational hospitality agents to be your frontline staff. They are not brain damaged, but they are going to have to deal with the flaming SOB that comes in who is raging and out for blood, behaviorally challenged, and coming for your throat. This picture is not a pretty one, but it's a true example of what can occur. For us to gain a better understanding of the rationale of customers' behavior and the challenge of dealing with them, let's look at the different types.

**Ego-centered Edward.** Edward has an ego the size of Alaska. His life is the main scene for everyone on earth. He is condescending, always right, and always the best. "Stand in line! Get behind me!" "Excuse me; I'm in a hurry here!" "Coming through!" He's always in a hurry for whatever he wants to purchase, even though he doesn't need it for another month.

**Excited Elena.** "Wow! This stuff looks great! How interesting. Are these available today? Go right ahead and help them I'll just keep looking, I can wait!" Never knowing exactly what they want, they're a salesman's dream. Find their buying motives and watch them walk out the store with a sale.

**Attacker Alice.** Does her ranting feel personal? Don't worry, it isn't. That's just how she is. Alice's attitude is the nastiest offense. Her language goes off the chart. Her vocabulary is shameful. She's commonly called Ms. Coupon Clipper. She's always out for the best deal, and you're always the lousiest person. She's caustic, crude, cruel, and absolutely foul mouthed to get what she wants. If things don't go exactly her way she's telling 50 friends not to shop at your store.

**Fresh Air Franny.** "Hi there, I could use some help. I've done some research and I thought you might be able to help me pick out the right one. Since you're the expert, can you answer a few questions for me?" She's very patient and very understanding, knows what she wants, and relies on the salesperson's expertise to help her make her decision. She likes the special one-on-one caring of a sales associate. Treat her right and she'll buy from you forever.

**Irrational Ira.** He's a screamer. Ira speaks before he thinks. He absolutely believes that he needs to grease the wheel with hate to get his refund or whatever else he wants. The more who are watching, the happier he is. He's cheap. He throws temper tantrums. He expects you to fix everything even though he wants to only pay for one thing. If you open your mouth once, he gets louder and louder and louder and starts over and over and over again. Hunker down, listen, don't say a word, don't react, don't take it personally, and when he's done, apologize and offer a solution.

**Emotional Emma.** "I'm a very sensitive and feeling soul. I like to get to know you and your family, personal things about you so we could bond. I make my decisions on how I feel. I give you trust and loyalty. I seek acceptance; however, if you stab me in the back or treat me wrong or put one over on me I will get you back. I'm what you call the silent majority. If you don't monitor my body language and if you don't ask me for feedback, I'm going to tell everyone I know how terrible you are, and you'll never see me again."

**Analytical Al.** "I know what I'm looking for when I come in. I've researched it, I've picked it out, and I know the details, so all I need you to do is to show me where it is. I need you to be accurate. I need you to answer any question I ask with the correct knowledge. I need to know that you have great ability and great information about the products I seek. I need you to be honest with me. Don't hurry me. Don't force me to make a decision. I take my time. If you allow me to do these things, then I will buy from you. However, if you cheat me out of one dime, I will make you feel intellectually puny and stupid and fight for my dime. You will lose my business if you don't handle it properly."

**The Bruce Willis.** This is one of your most diehard customers. They will be there with you through thick and thin, singing your praises to anyone who will listen. Treat these customers with utmost respect, and be very grateful for them. When you see them in the store, drop to your knees and say a quick note of thanks.

**The Entitled.** We've all dealt with these types of people, both in and out of our professional lives. They think the world is owed to them. You may as well roll out the red carpet when you see them pull into the parking lot. Nothing satisfies them, and you can't do anything right. When dealing with these types, be patient, remain calm, and don't argue. After all, you know you won't win, so let them take their time and eventually they'll make a decision.

**The Grab and Go.** Take a picture when you see this customer because they get in, get what they want, and get out. It is almost as if they just drank a bottle of water and have to go to the bathroom really bad. Head up, eyes on the prize, arms to the side, speedwalking to their destination. Don't take it personally if they don't answer you; they know what they want and don't have time to waste.

**The Inquisitive Five-Year-Old.** Have you ever taken a small child to the movie or watched TV with them before? If you have, then you know that every three seconds you're going to get a question. Their favorite phrases start with "Why? How come? When? What for?" Be patient and respond to their requests with politeness. Give them the information they request. Make the information customer focused. After all, this purchase is an investment for them, so try to look at it from their point of view.

Regardless of the type of customer you have, you need to develop a good working relationship with them all. The same basic principles of creating a good relationship apply to all customers, no matter what the personality type. Understanding the various types of customers helps to transform even the most difficult and demanding to loyal and dependable. Knowing these people can prove to be a huge advantage; knowledge is power.

## So How Do You Do as a Hospitality Hero on a Scale of 1–10?

- How effective were you with solutions to the different types of customers? _____

- How effective were you with dealing with their emotional ups and downs? _____

List three things that you can do to be effective as a hospitality hero to these types of customers:

1. _____

2. _____

3. _____

## Operator, May I Take Your Call?—Raise Your Intuitive Antenna

Through the endless lines of fiber optics, through the endless space of radio waves, an operator connects with heart and soul, and the ability to connect and make a friend. An operator's motto is listen, apologize if necessary, and solve the problem.

In face-to-face situations, it is easy to interpret someone's body language and facial expression and know instinctively how they are feeling. But if you are talking to them on the phone or via email, you still have to be able to recognize the different types of customers just by listening. Communication is vital when it comes to these types of interactions. You must communicate at every level. This includes their expectations of you, the company, and their purchase. Learning to communicate quickly with your customers by gaining an understanding of voice intonations gives you a significant competitive edge.

One of the greatest problems to effective communication with clients is the one-sided nature of speaking. Communication is not a one-way process. Let your customer express their opinions, concerns, and enthusiasm. Exchange between you and them is essential to effective, efficient, and accurate communication. Remember that listening is more important than talking. When you listen, you learn; when you talk, you learn nothing about whom you are communicating with. When you listen to your customers, keep the following in mind:

- **How your customer speaks.**

- **The words and phrases they choose.**

- **Their interests.**

- **Making sure both you and your client have the same expectations for delivery and quality of the service. (You both desire the same outcome.)**

Remember, the gift of gab isn't enough; you also have to know how to use it. To successfully communicate with different personalities requires specific skills. Understand your clients. It is very important to understand that each customer has a different background and their own style and preference for communicating. Don't judge your clients based on any preconceived notions, and keep an open mind. The best way to get to know your customers and what they want is to let them talk. Whether it's on the phone, in person, or via email, you will soon learn how to tailor your communication skills to fit their personality. Don't expect to immediately understand them within minutes of your first meeting, but do look for anything you can both relate to or for common ground. This is an important part of making a connection and often takes time and patience. Once you acknowledge common ground, they will convey their trust in you, and you can better communicate with one another.

Speak with eloquence. Your communication skills determine how people perceive you. Express your thoughts and feelings clearly. When you talk, be as clear, concise, and to the point as possible, based on your customer's needs. Don't waste the customer's time. Plan what you want to say and make sure they completely understand your message. Have something to say. Don't assume just because you're talking that your customers are listening. If you blurt out whatever comes to your mind, then they won't place much emphasis on anything you say. Keep meetings and conversations short, professional, and to the point.

Pay attention and be observant. This is not the same as listening. When you pay attention to your customers, they feel you have a deep understanding for their needs and what they are trying to say. Pay attention to your customer's tone of voice, a possible meaning behind the words, and any emphasis and hesitations. Go with your gut. Use your intuition to get a true sense of what your customers are telling you. View them with an open mind and try to get a sense of what this experience is like from their point of view.

Finally, have a good working rapport. Relax and smile. Always use a friendly tone of voice when you speak. Always have a positive attitude. A good rapport is best and most effective when both you and your client know each other's possibilities in the dialogue. Use humor appropriately, never at the expense of the customer. Acknowledge everyone's viewpoints and ideas. Your goal is to create the impression you're someone who is easy to work with, even if you must deal with serious issues or problems when they arise.

Your frontline employees are the best resource for discovering what your customers want, and they can best communicate with customers because they have the best access. Make communication skills mastery and conflict management a job requirement. Train, motivate, and encourage them to have conversations with customers that result in your company learning more about what your customers want. This helps your employees connect with customers and learn what they want and why they shop with your company. Again, feedback is vital.

## Action Steps

1. Develop a training that describes the different personality traits to your associates. (Or better yet, hire us!) Or have a program brought in.

2. Ask your staff to take the personality test in this chapter.

3. Practice communication within several different scenarios with your staff and then ask for feedback on the interaction. Role playing using a flip video camera is a useful process for getting good feedback.

# Chapter 4

## I Know That You Know

The old adage "When you assume, you make an ass of you and me" is particularly true regarding the needs and wants of customers in the marketplace today. The worst mistake you or your associates can make is to assume you know what a customer wants. One of the best examples of this involves an instance we heard at one of our seminars. A car salesman walked alongside a young couple looking to buy a car. After a few minutes of exchanging pleasantries, the three made their way toward the SUVs. As they walked, the salesman told them about the benefits and then made the fatal mistake of saying, "These units have an exceptional safety rating which I know you'll like, especially since you have a baby on the way." Seemingly harmless, right? Wrong; the lady wasn't pregnant. Needless to say, he didn't make the sale.

So if we are not able to act on our assumptions, how do we find out what customers want? In the tradition of one of our all-time favorite late night talk shows, we've come up with the Top Ten Ways to *Not* Get inside Your Customer's Head.

**10. Send relentless messages and friend requests on Facebook.**

**9.  Invite yourself to dinner.**

8. Bug their house.

7. Head-butt them in the hopes that information is transferred through osmosis.

6. Peep into their dining room windows during dinner and eavesdrop on their conversation.

5. Harass family and friends into providing private information.

4. Hire a private dick—we recommend Magnum P.I.

3. Call their mother.

2. Become their "Secret Admirer."

1. Don't worry about what they want. Customers are a renewable resource.

## 2–4–6–8—ALL of Your Customers are Great

The simplest, most basic reality of business is that unless you have customers, you do not have a business. Before you sweep the floors, empty the trash, or restock inventory, keep in mind that your first job is to connect with your customers with timely, helpful advice, and make them feel as if *they* are *your* number one priority. Advertising, slogans, branding yourself, and cutting costs are all methods we've used at one time or another to attract new and loyal customers. But those methods only have a short-term effect, if any. By truly understanding our customers, we are able to offer products and services that fit their specific needs, rather than pushing them toward our predetermined solutions not made for their individual circumstances.

All industries have one aspect in common with which they're constantly faced: the issue of finding and establishing loyal customers. That's why everyone, from sole proprietorships to corporate conglomerates, spends loads of time and money trying to make their companies "customer focused" or "customer-centric." In the majority of instances, all that time and money doesn't get the job done. Sadly, far too often, customers don't get enough individual attention and leave a business, frustrated and annoyed.

Understanding your company's brilliance and areas for opportunity is essential to your company's success. Give some attention to what your competition is doing—but concentrate on Y.O.U. (Your Opportunities Unlimited). Your Success Coach, Inc. has gained the knowledge, by studying the experts and becoming experts in developing the best tools and techniques, to learn how to get to know customers, identify their needs, and determine how to fulfill them. This is an integral part of the "Diamond Rule™" process we have created. Over the course of our research, we've also discovered the following three steadfast truths about customers:

• **Technology is fabulous when it works but stinks when it doesn't. This is true for both you and your customer. Computer-automated systems and advanced communications technology are a necessity in business today, but when Mr. Roboto decides to take a day off, life turns to chaos. Your customers don't care if your hard drive is fried or your email got spammed. Blah blah blah; these are just excuses to them. They also don't like to have to press pound key three hundred times to find out how much they owe. They are even angrier that the option to press "zero" anytime is gone. Sales representatives who don't have the slightest idea how to answer your questions, being placed on eternal hold, and constant website maintenance and downtime are not only inexcusable but almost guarantee a lost customer. No matter how complex the question, the process of getting to the right person with the right answer must be clear and simple.**

- Customers always surprise you. Never base your treatment on appearance or first impression. Bob Dylan was right: the times they are a-changin', and the conventional wisdom about what customers want and certain stereotypes are wrong. This reminds us of the sitcom *The Beverly Hillbillies*. After a first glance at Jed Clampett, would you think he was an oil tycoon? Better yet, the example we used earlier from the movie *Pretty Woman* with Julia Roberts and Richard Gere—Julia's character walked into the store on Rodeo Drive dressed in hooker attire only to be refused service, and was delighted to return a day or so later dressed to kill while waving her hidden elegance and newfound prosperity in the clerks' stunned faces. We had a similar experience in an exclusive women's clothing boutique in Richmond, Virginia. We walked into the store directly after playing tennis, looking awful. We were searching for a dress for a wedding. No one even acknowledged our presence. Our best friend was on her way from her job at a bank to help us (dressed to the nines). When she walked into the boutique she was immediately greeted by several associates. She said, "Don't look at me, they are the ones buying," and then pointed to us. The moral of all of these stories is, *make no assumptions* about the appearance of someone entering the doors of your business. It will cost you more than you can imagine.

- What is little to you may be huge to them. Never underestimate the power of the human touch. A small gesture or word makes all of the difference between a satisfied or angry customer. Talk to your customers as you want to be talked to. Some would argue that it is impossible to put a dollar value on the words "Please" and "Thank you." We disagree; if you don't already say those words to your customers, do so, and look at your bottom line. Without a doubt, you'll see an improvement. There is no business tool more powerful than the simple act of expressing your gratitude and appreciation with your customers. It's all about hospitality.

## Get a Clue

If you believe that your customers will continue to walk through your front door or click on your website because of competitive pricing, think again. It is personally directed, value-added services such as customer hospitality that earn loyalty. Pull into any biker bar across the country, and you'll most certainly see a parking lot full of Hogs. No, we don't mean pigs; we're referring to Harley-Davidson motorcycles. Once inside, the number of Harley tattoos rivals the number of bikes outside. Harley-Davidson's customers don't just admire them; they love their product so much they've etched its logo onto their biceps, knuckles, and chest and even named their children after their beloved bikes.

The Harley-Davidson logo is so popular and endearing, not only with Harley-Davidson motorcycle fans but with fashion connoisseurs alike, that it appears on T-shirts, belt buckles, and shoes; in fact, the popularity of the logo has created its own market of devout collectors. Is your company adored by fans across the globe? Are there letters of thanks and praise from customers who can't stop raving about you framed on your wall? If you answered no to one or both of these questions, then maybe it's time you do a bit of detective work and search for clues as to what's causing the issue and how we can improve.

So the main question we need to ask ourselves is, "What are you not doing with your customers that you ought to be?" Do you offer them 24-hour service? A live person to speak to? Does your product or service come with an unconditional guarantee? How do your quality, delivery, and price compare to your competition? What do your customers value most now and several months or years later? How does this perceived value relate to that of your competitors?

If you want to open a business, it makes sense to find someone who is already successful in that field and duplicate their performance, personalize and improve upon what they're doing, and make it your own. There is no need to reinvent the wheel. Using others' successes as a guidepost for your business saves time and shortens your learning curve. The same is true with customer hospitality. Investigate your competition and find out what they are doing, what they're offering, and what type of feedback they're receiving. After you've found the answers, look at your current and prospective customers, and outperform your competition. Always be willing to go the extra mile and offer more than those around you and more than the customer could ever expect.

Let's take our example. We knew that we wanted to venture into business consulting. So the first action we took was to research the most successful organizations. After inquiring about their services, we made a list of what they did and didn't do, as well as how they could improve. From this information, we put together our own business plan and made certain it exceeded our competitors'.

People expect a high degree of customer hospitality. You, as the provider, must be able to respond and deliver above and beyond their expectations—every time. Additional services, such as flexibility, timeliness, courtesy, accessibility, accuracy, and product knowledge, add to the customer's perceived value. Another bonus: these items don't cost you anything! The bottom line is that you either satisfy your customers' or someone else will. We have an excellent Client Feedback Form at the end of the chapter that you can copy and use.

## Follow Your Instincts

Malcolm Gladwell's book *Blink* opens with the story of an ancient Greek statue that came on the art market and was about to be purchased by the Getty Museum. We love this book because it discusses in detail the power of thought in decision making. The asking price for this statue was a little less than $10 million. With a price tag like this, you'd expect the museum to conduct extensive background checks to verify authenticity. They did, and a geologist determined that the marble came from the ancient Cape Vathy quarry because it was covered with a thin layer of calcite (a substance that accumulates on statues over hundreds or perhaps thousands of years). After more than a year of investigation, the Getty staff concluded the statue was genuine and moved forward with the purchase.

But don't make any plans to hop a plane to Los Angeles just yet. As Paul Harvey says, "And now, the rest of the story." An art historian named Federico Zeri traveled to see the statue, and in an instant he decided it wasn't real. While another expert looked at it, he sensed that while the form was correct, the work somehow lacked spirit. Also, he felt a wave of "intuitive repulsion" when he first laid eyes on it. Further investigations were made, and finally it was discovered that the statue had been sculpted by forgers in Rome. The teams of analysts who did the fourteen months of research were wrong. The historians who relied on their initial hunches were right: the statue was a fake.

Intuition has many definitions and descriptions. If we want to get technical, intuition is actually the act or faculty of knowing without the use of rational processes; immediate cognition, belief. Precursors include the Latin *intueri*, "to look at or toward, contemplate"; the Middle English *intuycion*, "contemplation"; and the Latin and French roots *in*—"inside" and *tuicion*—"to watch, guard, protect." Call it what you want, a hunch, a lucky guess, or a gut feeling, it is a specialized source of information that thousands of years ago people understood as a source of protection. Intuition is knowing without knowing how you know. Intuitive people appear to have a sense of more ultimate control and advantages in life because intuition and right-brain functioning add creativity, humor, and the ability to solve problems, to reach goals, and to manage people more effectively.

If we learn to listen deeply enough, intuition reveals significant, profound insights into any question we hold in mind. Every person has a process for evaluating the situations or events that occur in their life. Stop for a moment and think about the times you had a strong feeling about a customer who walked into your business or called you on the phone. Have you ever had a customer who you just knew was going to be difficult to deal with? So, based on this instinct, you approached them with caution and treated them with the best of customer hospitality. How were your results? In all reality, your instinctive actions defused a potentially ugly scenario. We all have flashes of intuition, but many of us ignore or distrust them as irrational and useless distractions.

Today, more than ever, we live in a global market and the competition is fierce. This emerging marketplace is placing tremendous pressure on business to adopt nontraditional methods of hospitality where success is not determined by a set of rules made by companies that succeeded in the past. Market research, demographics, and customer surveys give you important numbers, but don't have the personal connection so many of us are looking for today. When pie charts and spreadsheets don't give you enough information, intuition can provide a much better answer than crossing your fingers and making a guess.

Customers are most influenced by what they feel when they talk to sales associates. People buy from 80 percent emotion and 20 percent logic. Basically, they buy on how they feel. They want to buy; we just have to treat them well. Just imagine what would happen if you could train your employees to tap into these feelings. Intuition isn't some woowoo skill used only by gurus. We all have intuition, and the older we get, the more we trust it. A good way to start is to ask yourself, does it smell right, feel right, fit right? Thousands of successful managers and executives make business decisions using their intuition. Donald Trump, Oprah Winfrey, and Conrad Hilton are just a few examples of executives who have relied heavily on making intuitive business decisions.

Conrad in particular is famous for his "Connie hunches." In a real estate deal on a New York property, there was to be a sealed bid. Hilton evaluated its worth at $159,000 and prepared a bid for that amount. The next morning after he woke up, the figure of $174,000 stood out in his mind. So, he changed the bid to reflect the higher amount and it won. (The next highest bid was $173,000.) He subsequently sold the property for several million dollars.

Many other high-level executives admit that intuition has played a part in their success as well. This is rapidly becoming a critical skill necessary for success today. In a Burson-Marsteller Survey, 62 percent of CEOs use their gut feelings when making decisions. Intuition gives employees the ability to determine their customers' wants and needs before they even speak. Why is this so important? Simple: because it gives you leverage over your competition, and this is your secret ingredient to long-lasting success and loyal clientele.

In our brains, there are two parts: the thinking mind and the feeling mind. The feeling mind works to filter huge amounts of information, blend data, isolate telling details, and come to astonishingly rapid conclusions. Intuition is no different than exercising: in the same manner it takes time to build your body's muscles, it also takes time to build your mental muscles. Just as there is a relationship between exercise and strength, there is one between success and intuition. Douglas Dean, a researcher at the New Jersey Institute of Technology, studied this correlation and found that 80 percent of executives whose companies' profits had more than doubled in the past five years had above-average precognitive, intuitive powers.

If you truly want to master customer hospitality, you need to become more conscious of your intuitive faculties, and you need to start using them in a more systematic manner. Intuition can do much more for you than help you find out what your clients want. It can also help you integrate those answers so that you can use them to change your attitude and actions toward them. People don't want sales associates to placate them; they want informative answers based on knowledge. Intuition allows you to make the right decision quickly, even without all the facts.

Intuitive messages come in numbers of ways. They can come when you experience a hunch, a realistic dream, a vision, or just have a big fat "aha" moment. They can be expressed through the body when you experience tightness in one or more definitive body areas, when you notice a distinct change in energy, when you hear a helpful directive (from self-talk) or have specific awareness of changed feelings in a situation. For example, the feeling of tightness in your stomach, chest, or jaw could be your intuition speaking to you.

Because customer hospitality or suckiness (depending upon the situation you're in) is often chaotic, rational forms of decision making are often impossible, especially when heightened emotions are involved. So we need to be able to fall back on our intuition. Throughout our consulting, we've discovered that by using intuition, you'll always be R.I.G.H.T.™

- **Reason. Don't try to find a reason for your feelings. Just accept them and move forward.**

- **Idiotproof. There are no mistakes in intuition.**

- **Go for it. Intuition takes action.**

- **H**ard work. Intuition must be developed. It takes commitment and dedication to acknowledge and follow through with your instincts.

- **T**enfold. How much your profits can increase from relying on and teaching your staff to use intuition.

Those who accept the use of intuition in business do so in many ways. It is used in decision making, in product development, in stress management, in team building, in worker relationships, and in multiple other ways. As people begin to see work as a place for human, personal development, they begin to see deep intuition as key to that growth. They begin to use intuition to uncover and actualize the limitless potential of their lives.

As the rate of change and volume of information accelerate, analysis alone is often too slow a process to be effective. Many times, it is the hunch that defies logic, the gut feeling, or the flash of insight that brings the best solution. Those professionals who are both highly cognitive and highly intuitive have a distinct advantage in meeting challenges and solving problems. To develop your business intuition, begin by keeping a journal. Use it to capture your ideas, observations, and perceptions. Write down your dreams, feelings, and hunches. If you are going into a business meeting with people you haven't met, guess how they'll look and how they'll approach the business they plan to conduct. Record your gut feelings and keep a record of decisions you make on that basis. Check back occasionally to see which of your hunches were correct. By keeping score, you will be able to evaluate and increase your accuracy and profits.

# Action Steps

Identify "moments of truth" (where the engagement process was a success) for the next 30 days with both internal and external customers. Write them in your journal.

Write in your journal EVERY DAY—even if it's just a sentence on subjects like

> a. Actions you took that day
>
> b. Proud moments
>
> c. New ideas
>
> d. Stream-of-consciousness thinking

# Client Feedback Form

Please rate, on a scale of 1–10, these areas:

How effective was the engagement of the associate and were they attentive to your needs? Rate: _____

If it's not a 10, how can we become a 10?

_____

_____

_____

_____

Ability to purchase correct product or service. Rate: _____

If it's not a 10, how can we become a 10?

_____

_____

_____

_____

List up to three things we did that you liked and were very effective from your perspective:

_____

_____

_____

_____

List up to three things that we could do differently to ensure your continued support and patronage:

_____

_____

_____

_____

*Thank you for your feedback!*

# Chapter 5

Fat, Drunk, and Stupid Is No Way to Go through Life

We've all heard the phrase "You can't judge a book by its cover," but in customer hospitality, this isn't really the case. You can't judge your customers, but they can judge you. We know this sounds a bit hypocritical: here we are, telling you not to judge your customers, but almost in the same breath, we add that you need to be prepared to be judged by them. Customers tend to gravitate toward a person or a group of people or firms they like. Perception is in the eye of the beholder, and in a nanosecond, you're prejudged by each of your customers. We've spent over twenty years working in the customer hospitality industry, and too many of the clients we've worked with made bad first impressions because of one simple error—they forgot that the job wasn't about them. Don't take your bad day out on the customers. Suck it up and put a smile on your face. The bottom line about first impressions in the customer hospitality industry is that it doesn't matter if you have a bad day. It only matters if the customer has an exceptional day with you.

So if you've hired a group of misfits who look like they took their cousins to the prom, or smug associates who think they know it all, realize this decision reflects on you, too. Customers not only look for friendly knowledgeable help; they also want to feel comfortable around an associate. Someone who reeks of cigarette smoke, has on a dirty uniform, or maybe just has bad personal hygiene doesn't exactly make the interaction comfortable. It takes just a quick glance for someone to evaluate an associate and get a first impression. In this short time, they form an opinion based on appearance, demeanor, mannerisms, and behavior. What type of impression do you think your customers see when they walk into your business?

As a matter of fact, it goes a bit deeper than that; as an employer, manager, or executive, you're judged by your associates. Some people are scared to meet people. (These should not be your frontline associates.) They shiver and shake, sweat in a fully air conditioned room, or grit their teeth, taking a deep breath in between. Have you ever talked to a person standing behind the counter who sounded like a recording? They give you one-word answers like "Yes" and look like a frightened animal. You can't hide this type of fear; customers sense this and then become uncomfortable themselves.

Bad first impressions are also caused by anxiety. An anxious associate cannot think of something to talk about, and so they talk about what they know best: themselves. News flash: customers don't care about sales clerks' hobbies, how big their stereo system is, or what they had for lunch. One instance when we were at an electronics store comes to mind. While we were checking out buying a new laptop, the Dork Squad sales clerk shared with us that he thought laptops were useless. He was a professional gamer and only used desktops. By the time we left, we learned that he was going to complete four master's degrees in 18 months, that he already had six other master's degrees, and that he was retired. He only did this job for fun. Now, he was the only clerk available and had a huge line behind us of anxious customers. Do you think any of this mattered to us or the customers? Hell no! All we and everyone else in the eternal line cared about was getting out of there. Training your sales force to be relaxed and calm in the presence of customers is a necessity if you want to create lasting relationships and increase your bottom line.

Screw up a first impression, and you may not be able to repair the damage. The first time you meet a customer, you've got to create a positive and lasting impression all in ten to 20 seconds. This advice fits for every type of business in this world. We think that it will create a good impression with our customers, but the truth is, it creates frustration. Any conversation with your clients must not revolve around a single person, except the customer. We must not talk only about ourselves, and also we must not use the word "I." It's a dangerous word in conversation. Instead of using "I" use "We." It includes both or more persons, and also creates an impression of caring. You should let others discover who you are by their own initiative. Just because they shook your hand doesn't mean they want to attend a reading of your autobiography.

Speaking of handshakes, this is one of the most important indications of your staff's confidence level. Do the members of your staff have good ones? Many do not have a handshake. Instead, they hold out their hand for you to squeeze. While you may sense some body heat, that is the only sign of life apparent in the proffered limb. The arm muscles do not join in the shaking process; the fingers do not grasp your hand. Instead the handshake feels about as lifeless as plate of sautéed zucchini. Too strong a handshake, on the other hand, may leave you feeling like you've just shaken Mike Tyson's hand on a bad day. Remember, it's never a good idea to hear knuckles pop during a handshake. Also, beware of ladies wearing jewelry. A tight squeeze can ram a stone or sharp edge into her fingers. Another helpful hint: a handshake should never make a person's fingers bleed. Bad handshakers drive good handshakers nuts; it's as if they just go through the motions of meeting someone, while they think about something, or someone, else. A good handshake must be strong and steady, which gives customers the impression that you are confident and able to help them with their needs. A handshake is like a good cup of coffee, not too strong and not too weak.

So then what happens when your staff is too confident? The same: your customers are turned off and won't come back. This occurs when associates think their best way to make an impression on others is to show how smart they are. This mistake invariably makes you look eccentric,—or worse, it makes you look like Cliff Clavin from *Cheers*. Remember how annoying he was? He had an anecdote for every occasion. All of his little-known facts drove everyone crazy. Even if you are very bright, you will throw people off if you have a lot to say about every subject; others will become scared to talk, for fear of looking foolish.

Of course, physical appearance matters too. A picture is worth a thousand words, and so the "picture" you first present says much about you to your customers. Think about your reaction if you go to a restaurant and your server's hair is greasier then the fried chicken you ordered. The customer you are meeting for the first time does not know you, and your appearance is usually the first clue they have to go on. Are we saying you need to wear Armani suits and look like a model to create a strong and positive first impression? No, the key to a good impression is to present yourself appropriately for the job you are doing with confidence, self-assurance, humility, and caring about the person you're about to engage.

If you're going to dress like a stripper, than you'd better be swinging on a pole, because business dress doesn't include a whale tail. Just in case you're wondering, this is when a person's thong sticks out of the back of their pants. This advice isn't just for women, either. For you guys out there who think it's cool to go commando, please, for all of our sakes, don't wear low-rise jeans, or, if you do, have the decency to wear a belt. A friend of ours works at a local call center that he affectionately calls Butt Crack Central. What's in style today doesn't always make the best work attire. Also, dress appropriately for your body type. Why is it that people who frequent all-you-can-eat buffets, if you get our drift, think they can wear tube tops, miniskirts, and low-cut clothes? These types of fashion faux pas are nothing more than distractions for not only your customers but other employees as well.

Along with appropriate dress, you need to be clean, too. We can't believe that this even needs mentioning, but unfortunately there are those in this world who don't believe in daily showers and deodorant. Brush your teeth and make sure your breath stays fresh throughout the day. If you have halitosis, use a breath freshener frequently. You'll know if you've failed at this if your customers are constantly backing away from you. Make sure your hair is brushed and you have cleared your eyes of the sleepy-eye gunk. Your customers should never feel like they need a gas mask to shop in your store. Your dress and grooming should always, not sometimes, make a good first impression and should also help you feel "the part." As a result you'll act more calm and confident. With every new encounter, you are evaluated and yet another person's impression of you is formed. These first impressions can be nearly impossible to reverse or undo, making those first encounters extremely important, for they set the tone for the all the relationships that follow. Always remember that first impressions count for a lot; walk into the interview with your head held high, smile, and give a firm handshake. Showing you have confidence in yourself is essential and can make all the difference to you being successful.

## Thank You Sir. May I Have Another?

First impressions are all the information that customers see or learn about you. Initially, when someone sees such a small piece of an employee, that is all they know about them and the business, for that matter. No matter how great a product or service you offer, how clean the store is, or how reasonable the prices are, if a client walks in and some small behavior rubs them the wrong way, they may never shop there again. We can recall several times in our lives when we've walked out of a store and stated, "We can't believe what just happened—we're never coming back!" And we never did.

There are certain behavioral norms that we are expected to use during the course of regular interactions with other people. Not burping, passing gas, picking your nose, and so on is just common sense.

Etiquette is an important part of everyday life, and our manners while engaging with customers are just as important. Business etiquette, however, is more than knowing to put your napkin in your lap and goes far beyond not belching in the boardroom. It's about projecting an image of professionalism and credibility. This skill is necessary to develop and sharpen your business communication skills to enhance both your professional image and promotability. Good manners and business etiquette have always been based on common sense and thoughtfulness. It is about presenting yourself in a manner that demonstrates you can be taken seriously as well as being comfortable around people and making them comfortable around you, too.

How you act affects the people around you. Being nice to people is proven to make you feel better and boost morale, so it's a good way to start the day off right. The Cardinal Rules start with

- Putting people at ease.

- Adapting to their behaviors.

- Getting them talking about themselves and keeping them talking.

- Being attentive.

- Making them feel important.

- Using following skills—asking open-ended questions.

- Making them feel heard.

- And last but not least, reflecting—give them back a chunk of what you heard and make them feel understood.

Any behavior perceived as disrespectful, discourteous, or abrasive is easily avoided by using good business etiquette. Customers are a major player in your business's success. Unfortunately, many potentially worthwhile and profitable relationships have been lost because of an unintentional breach of manners. We've always found that most negative experiences with someone were unintentional and easily repaired by keeping an open mind and maintaining open, honest communication. Basic knowledge and practice of etiquette is a valuable advantage, because as mentioned earlier, you may not get a second chance to make a first impression.

Etiquette can occasionally be an ugly beast to tame, depending on the type of company, local culture, and the circumstances of the situation, but it behooves you to learn it *and* apply it to your dealings with customers. Cultural courtesy is becoming very important as more business is being conducted in and with foreign countries. Show appreciation and respect for the differences between our country and someone else's. Always be aware of and sensitive to their rules of etiquette. If you are traveling overseas representing an American firm, it is crucial to act in accordance with the customs and culture of the country you are visiting. This can be very important to your business dealings. Research the customs and culture of the country with which you will have business transactions.

No one's perfect, and chances are you'll make a mistake and offend someone, but we'll discuss how to defuse that situation a bit later in this book. The most important rule to remember in business is to be courteous and thoughtful to your customers, regardless of the situation. Consider other people's feelings, and stick to your convictions as diplomatically as possible. Put your clients at ease, and make them feel as though they had chance to say what they wanted and that you listened to them and responded to them sensitively. Treat people above and beyond their expectations. Business etiquette should be give-and-take, to help each other when help is needed and have consideration for others.

Politeness and courtesy set the tone for work relationships, how you interact with people, and how people perceive you. Etiquette issues will become even more important in the future as increasing racial, gender, and cultural diversity in the workplace makes it important for supervisors and coworkers to be sensitive to interpersonal dynamics and have respect for different communication and working styles.

Those are the simple rules of social etiquette in conversation. Remember five words that are too often neglected in business:

- **Please.**
- **Thank you.**
- **Great job.**

Social skills can help us build more productive relationships. In these changing times, we need to prepare for a variety of encounters in both the business and social environments. Your manners and etiquette are not just actions—they are an attitude—an attitude that is closely related to your self-confidence, your position in business and personal life, and your ability to build successful relationships, teams, and organizations.

Your associates are your company—they are a direct reflection of your brand. Do they represent you with polish, intelligence, and class? Mistakes in business etiquette can severely damage your associate's reputation and reflect poorly on you and your company. With the workforce becoming more diverse than ever, the chances of saying or doing the wrong thing are much greater than ever before.

Business etiquette training will give your associates the awareness and the skills to acquire key clients and cultivate lasting relationships. Whether or not your company makes the next sale depends on your associates' abilities in the following: face-to-face engagement, dining etiquette, email and phone etiquette, and how they dress at the next sales presentation. Business etiquette training will equip your associates with the tools they need to create customer intimacy and build effective relationships. Without achieving customer intimacy, we cannot build relationships that lead to rapport, trust, and credibility. Clearly, deeper relationships do matter to customers. Sales associates need to prepare differently, engage differently, and follow up differently. Learning and applying the Diamond Rule™ will give you a leg up on the competition.

# Action Steps

1. Make a list of all your past customer complaints.

2. Have a meeting with your employees and brainstorm ideas for solutions to those problems. Involve everyone in the decision making.

3. Write a list of ways to prevent future problems and post the list in the break room, bathroom, and any other area where your employees congregate.

# Chapter 6

## Smile, Even If You've Just Stubbed Your Toe

Recently, we went to our local post office to pick up a package. It must have been snowing in hell because there was no line. Anyway, a lady sitting behind the counter stared at us for a few minutes while she smacked her gum. It was almost like a showdown at the OK Corral. No words between the three of us. In the background, tumbleweeds swirled about and we could hear the distant howl of a coyote. The time was getting near; who was going to be the first to draw? Would we the customers have to speak first, or the leather-faced lass behind the counter? Ready, set, go. "Can I help you?" There was no enthusiasm in this women's voice. It sounded as though she had gargled with granola for the past twenty years. When we showed her the door tag for our package, you would have thought that we asked to borrow a hundred bucks. There is nothing more irritating then hearing a loud sigh or moan from an associate.

We were tempted to tell Gravel Gurdy to shove the package in a different mailbox, if you get our drift, but we didn't. Instead we waited for her to slither to the back and bring us our package. Once we had our box, we thanked her and told her to make it a nice day. To which she replied with a scowl, "My day won't be better until five o'clock."

No doubt that Gravel Gurdy was having more than just a bad day, but that's no excuse. If you're experiencing too much internal torment or have hatred for your fellow man, take a day off. Attitude is everything when it comes to customer hospitality. Now, we know that there are no perfect jobs and every one of us gets into a bad mood from time to time. You can and must choose self-control and self-correction and turn your attitude around. Listen to your self-talk or the way you talk to others. Do you snarl and use rude words? How about the way to speak to yourself? Do you tell yourself that you're not good enough or smart enough? Before you come into contact with any customers, get in a positive frame of mind. Your job may not be fun or meaningful; however, it is what you make of it. Make a decision about your job and your life, asking this question: How do you want them to be—fun and enjoyable, helping others, or drudgery and despair? If you don't maintain a positive attitude at work you'll

- **Lose your customers' respect and business.**

- **Decrease the overall morale among other associates.**

## B.U.G.S.

Have you ever eaten at a restaurant and noticed a roach or ant crawl across the floor, or worse, your table? We're willing to bet that hamburger didn't taste as good as before, that is, if you even stayed there long enough to eat. Bad attitudes are like those bugs in the diner. They are everywhere, difficult to get rid of, and can cause your customers to run out the door screaming. With bugs, if you've got one, it is only a matter of time before you'll see more. The same is true with bad attitudes. Because of this, we've developed this acronym.

- **Below-standard greetings.**

- **Unsatisfactory service.**

- Grumpiness
- Soured disposition.

Associates with bad attitudes destroy morale and turn off customers by talking and acting negatively. It's like the manager who asked his new secretary, "Can you please make me a copy of this report?" Her response was, "Are your hands broken?" Negative associates aren't willing to go the extra mile. They'll do just enough to get by and have little or no initiative. Comments such as "How much longer until five?" and "God, is it only 9:15? I feel like I've been here forever" are indicative of an associate with a lousy work attitude. Words aren't the only indication of a negative work attitude, either. Behaviors can be very telling. A friend of ours, Greg, went to get his oil changed after work one day. He pulled up to the bay and asked for some help. The associate told him that they were closed. Greg looked at his watch, which told him that it was ten to five. The man said, "Yeah, but we've already cleaned out our bays and we don't want to mess them up again." Greg was furious and used a few choice words and made a vow to never go to this oil change place again. This happened in 1999, and to this day, Greg hasn't set foot inside the business and still tells everyone the story.

How much business do you think those clean bays have cost the company over the years? As owners and managers, we can't afford to have negative, nonperforming associates on the payroll. The 3M Corporation discovered this during a layoff at one of their facilities. When management laid off the bottom 10 percent (their poorest performers) at one facility, their productivity skyrocketed up 18 percent. When they laid off another ten percent (the next poorest set of performers), productivity went up another four percent. That company learned that negative associates not only produce less, but also cost more.

Let's say that you have a situation in your company in which Darlene the Diva constantly stirs up the negativity through gossip, backstabbing, and complaining. The damage caused by Darlene is quick and powerful, but how much is the long-term cost? The more Darlene spouts her garbage, the more fed up her coworkers become. Finally, after having enough, three top producers leave, partially because of Darlene, but more because of management's refusal to deal with the situation. Each former associate earned over six figures a year. The cost of recruiting and training replacements is at least two times their annual salaries. Consequently, the cost of keeping Darlene on the job has exceeded one million dollars this year alone, and that does not include her salary and benefits.

Crappy attitudes increase turnover. People don't want to be around negative people or those who don't make them feel good. Once **B.U.G.S.** gets loose, associate morale plummets and there is a sense of "there has got to be something better" in the air. People also take more days off for longer periods of time, they're late more often, and you get increased customer complaints. The reasons management tolerates negative associates are too numerous to list here, but let us share one very important point: A negative associate never helps a company be more productive and profitable. Regardless of the reason why negative associate behavior is tolerated, there is a solution.

The solution isn't to transfer them to a different department or a different shift. This is no different than finding out you have the flu and giving your mother-in-law a kiss on the mouth. You've just infected the other associates with negativity and a bad attitude. Transferring someone doesn't help, because they bring their soured disposition with them. "Location, location, location" only applies to real estate. Is it possible to transform a negative attitude into a positive one? Do you have the power to make this happen? Yes you *can!*

## Feedback Is Vital

Sadly, we've found most of the people who are negative in the workplace don't know it. Why? They don't get the necessary feedback. Without an associate assessment tool like we offer with Your Success Coach, the solution is hit-or-miss. What specific skills were your associates expected to adhere to on a daily basis? Do associates know their job expectations? Not just for the week after they were hired but ongoing, forever and ever and ever, every day with every customer, whether on the phone or in front of them? Many times we've seen a negative associate's bad attitude tear through an organization, disrupting productivity, uprooting associates, and destroying morale everywhere, and they were completely oblivious.

How vulnerable is your organization to the effects of a negative associate and what are you doing about it? Is it possible to rebound from a negative attitude to become an outstanding associate? Yes, you *can!* First, you must take responsibility for your own actions. Second, acknowledge your bad attitude; look at and evaluate the feedback in an objective manner. Third, step outside your bruised ego and look at things from the perspective of your coworkers and employer. Finally, hold yourself accountable and personally responsible for your own actions and behaviors. Recognize that your behavior is not getting you what you want. If, for example, you want a raise, a promotion, or more responsibilities in your position, you need to improve your attitude and behaviors to achieve the targets you are aiming for. Give and receive feedback on a regular basis and keep the lines of communication open. Ongoing communication and feedback helps to prevent major issues later.

Despite the initial reaction, which may be negative, don't take it personally, and learn to be responsive rather than reactive. Maintain your composure following any feedback. Learn to manage and control your emotions. Being argumentative, name-calling, throwing tantrums, and a multitude of other unbecoming behaviors may feel good at the time, but are not qualities of a professional working adult. Look at all feedback as corrective or complimentary of your behavior and actions. Instead of screaming like a lunatic or pouting like a four-year-old, use the corrective aspects of the feedback to challenge yourself to do better, and look at it in a positive light. If your supervisor stated you don't take initiative on projects, seek opportunities to show you are able and willing to do so. Become the opposite of every negative aspect of your assessment. Choose to become a better asset to yourself, your company, and your customers. Reality is determined by your respecting your choice and decision to seek out opportunities.

Don't allow limitations to hold you back. Reality also is determined by your ability to respond to situations with control and objectivity. Don't react out of emotion and subjectivity. You can change the negative implications of your attitude for the better. You can rebound, raise your level of self-awareness, and become an exceptional associate who seeks out their genius and puts it to work. Do not be discouraged. Strive for excellence in achieving your full potential as a person and associate. For instance, we coached a client who was miserable in his job. As the company's vice president, he was more than qualified to do his job but nevertheless always felt inadequate and wasn't achieving the results he knew he was capable of. After working with him, we helped him realize that he wasn't working toward his strengths. Throughout our coaching, we also found out that he and the company's president didn't work well together. As a result, he left and started his own successful company. Another benefit is that the president is much happier, too, because he now has found someone he can work well with. This is just one of the many examples that Your Success Coach has of helping clients find their genius and play to their strengths.

## The Cycle

Our experience has taught us that an attitude that portrays confidence in yourself, and the demeanor to go along with it, attract people to you. Have you ever had a task to complete and you felt so confident you could do the job that you didn't give it much thought, only to have a negative member of your office come along and, with just one destructive comment, destroy your confidence? A few "harmless" observations can devastate morale and needlessly jeopardize your positive outlook, which is essential to complete the job in an exceptional manner.

Let's look at another scenario involving ineffective teamwork. We've all heard the phrase "One bad apple spoils the barrel." This is certainly the case in an office setting. Have you ever been a passive observer in a staff that housed a perennially negative person? When the group faces a problem, it doesn't matter who comes up with a solution or what their suggestion is; the pessimistic member of the group shoots it down or finds some problem with it. Eventually, that person will drive the solution into the ground, and leave the group collectively rolling their eyes at them. From that moment on, the group has less respect, maybe substantially so, for their coworker and will likely discount the vast majority of what they have to say. Whether you believe that a positive outlook can improve your chances of succeeding or not, negativity never does you any favors in the workplace.

We all know that our work environments can suck sometimes. Especially on Mondays, right? Walking in the door with a positive attitude and a smile will make even the tensest office bearable and a place where people can come to work without feeling stressed to the point that they are in their cars, jabbing seven different coworker voodoo dolls in the eyes with a paper clip before they clock in for the day. You'll find that an optimistic outlook and a smile are just as infectious as your counterpart's negativity. The feeling of spreading something besides the flu through your office will act as an additional motivating factor. Creating a positive work environment is something that everyone benefits from. Not only is break time more fun for the entire office, but the work is more fulfilling and easier to accomplish. You'll know that a positive attitude has successfully spread throughout your entire office when the climate has changed and the work environment becomes fun and much more pleasant.

Most associates agree that sometimes they don't have control over anything. There is one aspect of your work that you have complete control over—your attitude. Your attitude is your choice and your choice alone. Sometimes, as associates, we have to take every victory we can get, as small as it may be. Make the choice to feel good about your job and you will begin to feel better. Decide to be happy for no reason at all, and let it show.

It's important to make this conscious effort to change your attitude because you'll only make it as far as your attitude will allow you to go. If you're full of crippling self-doubt and negativity, then you will have trouble conjuring up the motivation to enact a change in yourself, never mind actually following through successfully with any of those changes. One way to look at the idea of positive attitude and success in your career is that one leads to another and back again. It's a cycle—positive thinking leads to success, which leads back to more positive thinking, and so on. This can be discouraging if you think you can't break your way into this self-fulfilling prophecy cycle. It should serve as more motivation to change your thinking and your prophecy. The momentum of experiencing success will lead even the most negative person to believe that they can repeat their success the next time out.

Maintain a positive outlook in every conceivable situation. There will definitely be times when your resolve is tested, but you can't lose that confident attitude that tells you that you can turn the situation around and make it all work in the end. When we deviate from an optimistic attitude, we risk moving away from a proven path of success. Imagine your manager challenges your team to sell 25 cars in a month. Let's say that that on the 25th day of the month, your team has only sold 14 cars. If you abandon your positive thinking, you've further stacked the deck against yourself. Instead, maintain your positive outlook, continue to listen to feedback, and make changes when necessary to get better results.

In order to keep moving forward, you have to envision yourself accomplishing all of your goals as planned. When you allow the negative feeling to enter into the equation, you've already made things harder for yourself. Why add a hurdle to an already challenging task, like having to also overcome your own negative emotions? In every situation, good or bad, stay positive. You can always find the good in every situation. Sometimes you just have to look harder. The decision about how you see it is yours. That will make reaching your ultimate goal easier to do than abandoning positive thoughts to unnecessarily make things harder for yourself than they have to be.

There is power in positive thinking, and utilizing that power will bring you results that are an improvement. As difficult as it may be to buy into the system, you will benefit from changing your thought process to make your professional tasks easier to achieve all the while helping to create a far happier, stress-reduced, and pleasant working environment.

## Be a Role Model, Be a Beacon, Walk the Talk

As professional speakers, we've had a good deal of experience talking in front of large groups of people. Your audience can literally make or break a good speech. The image of the comedian dying on stage comes to mind. If the audience is "with you," you have their undivided attention. They hang on your every word. They give you both verbal and nonverbal feedback. They nod their heads in agreement and smile or sometimes even give an OK or a thumbs-up sign. Or, they can do just the opposite. They can turn you off, avoid eye contact, start conversations of their own, and even actually get up and leave!

Each business has two audiences. The first audience is made up of your associates, who communicate with each other every day. This is good and bad in that they can and will mimic good and bad behavior, depending upon what they see you and other staff members doing. They will work hard for managers they respect and will put in only "necessary time" for those they do not respect. The second audience is your customers. Your associates also "play" to this audience. Many times the same "performance" that is done internally with their peers, is "delivered" to the customer. It can be one of excitement and genuine friendliness or it can be done grudgingly and with very little professionalism.

How are the associates you work with? Are they robots, unable to make eye contact or say two words without mumbling? Is there anyone who sets an example of how to act rather than how *not* to act? Who is the "role model" in your company? Who's the beacon? Who walks the talk? It had better be everyone from the CEO right down to the associate who sweeps the floors. You see, the associates are watching every move management makes, and they mimic what management does. Do you act as good a role model for customer hospitality? The importance of having a role model can never be underestimated.

If you set a good example for your associates, you'll more likely inspire them to work with, not against you. Like anyone else, associates can see what's wrong with a situation, but role models don't get stuck on a problem. They keep themselves motivated by seeing the good in any situation and focus on methods to make it better. By contrast, negative associates focus on a minor annoyance and let it ruin everything. Like a hangnail—picking and picking and picking at it until there's nothing left. It's like the associate who attended one of our workshops. Even though her company paid for the trip and program, the hotel was very nice, and the training was excellent, their only comment about the entire event was the fact that the chairs in the training room were too cold. Maybe they were, but the associate's focus on the air conditioning prevented them from learning from the seminar.

Every business owner or manager knows the Cardinal Rule in business is to underpromise and overdeliver. The same is true with associates who have positive attitudes. They're never satisfied with merely getting by or doing the bare minimum. They know if they were to do that, they couldn't possibly feel good about themselves. Optimistic associates find out what's expected and do their best to exceed those expectations. Whether it's wowing a customer with better than expected service, or offering a coworker a helping hand, positive associates focus on how they can do more, not less—how they can make someone else's day.

Your attitude is reflected in your customer. Your words should be encouraging and never demeaning. Stop for a moment and think back to a time when a store's representative talked down to you. We were shopping for a dining room table a while back, and overheard a conversation with a salesman and another customer. A young lady was looking for a sleigh bed and couldn't decide whether or not to buy a queen- or king-size frame. In a smug tone, the clerk said, "Do you even have a mattress?" Offended, she left the store. No one wants to be treated badly or talked to in a condescending tone.

Let's put the shoe on the other foot for a moment. Imagine you are in the market for a new car. You've spent a ton of time and energy researching and reading consumer reviews. This is a substantial purchase, and you're very excited. Now, what characteristics would you look for in an associate? Negative? Insecure? Low self-esteem?

Of course not. You would look for traits such as enthusiasm, pride, a good personality, and a positive attitude.

So what do your associates and customers really see? Do they see management devoted to creating and delivering a positive working environment and climate that guarantees they will receive the quality of products and service that the company has promised, every time, or is your internal or external customer hospitality infested with **B.U.G.S.**?

## Action Steps

**Ask your employees to complete the following attitude assessment:**

**What is the mission statement of the company?**

_____

_____

_____

_____

**What do think your position is within the company?**

_____

_____

_____

_____

**How do you think you contribute to the company?**

_____

_____

_____

_____

Do you feel you make a difference in the company? How? What specifically have you done? Give an example.

_____

_____

_____

_____

Are you actively involved in any decision making that directly affects your job? How, and with what types of decisions? Give an example.

_____

_____

_____

_____

Do you have ready access to the information you need to get your job done? Give an example of your training. Describe the training you need to be successful in your job.

_____

_____

_____

_____

Do feel that management has created an open and comfortable work environment? Give an example.

_____

_____

_____

_____

Do you feel that management recognizes and makes use of your abilities and skills? How? Give an example.

_____

_____

_____

_____

Do you know your job requirements and what is expected of your on a daily basis? How is your success measured?

_____

_____

_____

_____

Have you received the training you need to do your job efficiently and effectively? Give an example.

_____

_____

_____

_____

Are you encouraged to develop new and more efficient ways to do my work? How? Give an example.

_____

_____

_____

_____

Would you recommend that others work for this company? Why?

_____

_____

_____

_____

What changes, if any, do you feel need to be made in the company to improve working conditions?

_____

_____

_____

_____

# Chapter 7

## You Mean I Actually Have to Talk to Them?

In a galaxy far, far away, or at least that's what it seemed like, we changed our personal cell phone account into a business one for tax purposes. Every month after the switch, our bill was incorrect. We were guaranteed at the time the change was made our charges would be exactly the same as they were before. How foolish we were for believing them. To keep your word—to always tell the truth—what a novel concept. The only consistency on our bill was the inconsistency. So every month, we diligently called and explained our situation to one of any number of uncaring sales representatives. And every month, our new bill arrived, incorrect. We called again, explained our situation again, hoped it was resolved, and patiently waited for the next bill.

Second verse same as the first; you guessed it, the bill was wrong again. Yeah, we know, big surprise. In typical *Groundhog Day* fashion, we again dialed the phone and spoke with the first sales representative and explained our situation. But wait; there is more to the story. Apparently, neither of us were authorized agents on *our* account either. Hey, that's great. The young man on the other end of the line told us that we were not authorized agents, even though both of our names were on the bill. Irritated, we said,

"Well, that can't be. We opened this account personally and our names are on the bill." To which he responded, "Just because your name is on the bill doesn't mean you're an authorized agent on the account."

We both found this quite amusing, considering we were the only two people on the account to begin with. The young man on the other end of the phone, however, was not amused. We could do nothing. We could make no changes. As far as he was concerned, we were trying to make changes to an account that we had no authorization for. By this time, our blood pressure was boiling, those little veins in our foreheads were popping out, and our palms were to the point of bleeding from us making fists. We looked like two deranged Wonder Twins ready to activate into a weapon of mass destruction. We insisted that this issue be resolved. The young man explained to us that we would have to write a letter with certain pieces of information on it in order for us to become "authorized agents." This was completely unacceptable. We had had this account for almost eight years. The error was not ours. Why should we have to fix the problem?

To make matters worse, we would have to fax a letter to the company on our dime. Well, that was the last straw. We didn't ask to speak to the supervisor; we demanded. After we waited on hold for 23 minutes, a supervisor finally picked up the phone. Of course, Skippy Doodle didn't take any notes, so we had to explain the entire story all over again. After another frustrating 20-minute conversation we finally resolved the issues. We still had to fax the letter, but they were going to credit us money on our next bill. This was one of the largest wireless phone companies in the world, too!

This experience made us think about the old *Saturday Night Live* skit in which Lily Tomlin acted as Ernestine, the operator at the telephone company. One ringy dingy snort, two ringy dingy snort.

She either disconnected her caller or rerouted them to the wrong number. After listening to the caller rant and rave, she sheepishly said, "We're the telephone company; we don't care because we don't have to." Well, apparently no one informed our wireless phone provider that they have competition and that they should care.

The moral of this story is that no matter how amusing Ernestine's words were, they will not work in today's society. We guarantee you that as soon as we are finished with our contract with this company we will leave and go to a new one. They might not be as good or as big, but they will care more and try harder to keep our business. To paraphrase the immortal words of *The Incredible Hulk's* David Banner, "Don't make us angry; you won't like us when we're angry."

## And Then She Said Yada Yada Yada ...

If you're reading over the warranty of one of your products, you can just say "90-day replacement yada yada yada, initial here, yada yada yada, and sign here." To be successful, your business (and it doesn't matter if you sell seashells by the seashore or multimillion-dollar heating and air conditioning units) needs to communicate effectively with both your staff and customer base. Imagine, for example, what would happen if you placed an ad in the paper stating that your store will open at 6 AM for the big sale but didn't tell your employees that their workday started two hours earlier. Can you say "public relations nightmare"? How many customers would you lose? All of this could have been avoided by talking to your staff in a manner that they understood. Several keys to effective communication are to

- **Instruct staff on what to do to create customer hospitality and thus repeat business. "How are you today? Is there anything I may help** you with?" is much better than "Whatz up, do you need any help 'cause I'd really like to hop out back and take a smoke right now." Remember, customers like to work with knowledgeable staff who can confidently express themselves. Customers don't want to be sold to; however, they do like to buy from salespeople who care and know what they're talking about. That's why they're there.

- Keep staff informed of any new policies or changes in products so that they are able to perform their work in an excellent manner, taking care of the customers' needs and wants, and enjoy what they are doing. What if, for example, management sends a memo down ordering no more wearing jeans and you don't relay that appropriately. What happens when your territory manager conducts a surprise visit to a showroom full of salespeople in denim? Set them up for success with more information. Do not hold information back, setting them up for failure.

- Enable people at the same level within your business to communicate with each other. Share and share alike! Brainstorming at every level should be paramount over just one person's ideas. It encourages and expands on creativity. The more minds you have working, the more creative you can be. Masterminding creates a third mind that gives you limitless opportunities. The maintenance crew has to be able to communicate with the sales staff and vice versa. Ensuring that the different departments such as sales and production, for example, in your business can communicate makes the whole process run smoother and limits the amount of antacids you'll consume on a daily basis.

- Communicate openly with its suppliers, orders, shipments, and customers. This is vital for continuous incremental improvement. There are two methods that can be used for quality assurance and continuous improvement: the Deming Wheel we discussed in chapter two, and the Japanese process, *kaizen*, whose main goal is to eliminate any non-value-added activities and manufacture only what is needed by the customer, when it is needed, and in the quantities ordered. As with the Deming Wheel, kaizen has proven to shorten lead times, reduce work in process, and minimize the need for capital expenditures.

Exceptional communication skills are vital in being effective. They are vital for everyone from CEOs and upper- to mid-level management to frontline employees. How often have you felt that someone doesn't understand you, takes you for granted, doesn't take you seriously, and twists what you're saying? Do you have difficulty expressing yourself the way you want to express yourself? Most of us have experienced one or all of these feelings at some time or another. One of the main reasons for this is people don't realize that communication has two main parts—listening and talking. Receiving information and transmitting information. One of the most important aspects of communication is knowing how to be an exceptional listener and being able to adapt to the needs of those around you. Ninety-nine percent of selling is active listening.

Employees and supervisors sometimes feel as though they are speaking a completely different language. Still, listening to each other is important because this is the crucial to the overall success of the company. Active listening is a vital part of business. It is a communication tool that can help associates and management speak with each other clearly and be understood. Active listening is about focusing on the person who is speaking and their point of view. To demonstrate that you are actively focusing on your counterpart, you use the following three techniques.

**Following skills.** What we are referring to here is asking questions, prompting and encouraging them to continue sharing. The premise is get 'em talking and keep 'em talking! The more they talk, the more you learn. Following skills makes the person speaking feel heard. Often, questions can seem accusing or blaming to the person asked. A question may make the person feel backed into a corner. For example, if a supervisor asks their sales associate, "You didn't want to speak to that customer, did you?" it is clear that they don't approve of the way in which the customer was greeted. If, however, the employee did the best they could, they end up feeling the need to defend their position. Consider how much easier it would have been to respond to the question "What did you think of your greeting?" Ask open-ended questions that allow for a variety of responses. The use of "what" and "how" generates action-oriented responses. These are the best objective questions to ask when you're getting information. If you ask closed-ended questions, you limit the range of responses and suggest that you already know what is going to be said. To encourage people to express their opinion, rather than just regurgitating what they think their supervisor wants to hear, you can ask more questions to encourage further thinking.

Active listening requires the speaker to listen naively with no judgments or assumptions, to keep an open mind, and to look at the possibility of a hidden meaning behind the question. People often ask questions that might make others feel pressured into coming up with the correct response. For example, you might feel pressured when your boss asks you, "Do you think you're doing a good job?" These types of questions tend to put the person being asked on the defensive. Often they may shut off communication in order to protect themselves. In order to be a good active listener, you need to make sure that you ask questions honestly and sincerely, and that the intent behind questioning is to understand rather than advise, criticize, or pry. Through this process, associates will also understand their own thinking by fostering decision-making and planning skills.

When you use active-listening questions you can

- **Learn about others' thoughts, feelings, and wants: "Share with me more about your ideas for the project."**

- **Encourage elaboration: "What happened next?" or "How did that make you feel?"**

- **Encourage discovery: "What do you feel your options are at this point?"**

- **Gather more facts and details: "What happened before the customer left?"**

**Listen nonjudgmentally.** (attendant skills—listening with body language, making them feel important) Disregard any preconceived notions you may have about the person who is speaking. Ignore your own, adult perception of the situation for the moment and accept your employees' feelings, thoughts, and ideas of the situation as yours. See it through their eyes during your discussion. Don't dismiss what is being said as wrong or just plain stupid. Your acceptance of your associates' thoughts, ideas, and feelings increases the chance that they will talk to you about any current or future problems and issues.

**Paraphrase or reflecting.** Restate what your employee or supervisor just told you in your own words. This process makes the speaker feel understood. "So, for example, what you're saying is...." Paraphrasing is a tool you can use to make sure that you understand the message that you think your associates or boss is sending. It is restating the information you just received to make sure you understand it. This technique helps management and associates in several ways. First, it helps everyone make sure they understood the message correctly. Second, it helps management and associates draw further information from each other. Third, it allows the associate to know that management has heard them and is interested in what they have to say. Fourth, and we think most importantly, it allows for an opportunity to correct any misunderstanding immediately. Let's take a look at some examples of a few paraphrased dialogues (paraphrased responses are italicized):

"I hate this %$@#*, she is always so rude!" *"It sounds like you're having a hard time with Mrs. Smith. What does she do specifically to make you feel frustrated and uncomfortable?"*

"This job sucks. How come I always get asked to do the crap work?" *"So what you're saying is that you don't like this particular job and don't feel like you're a valued team member?*

Active listening takes time and practice and will not produce results overnight, so remember to watch out for the following listening barriers:

- **Forgetting the topic of discussion (going on vacation in your mind).**

- **Interrupting the speaker.**

- **Not maintaining eye contact with the speaker.**

- **Rushing the speaker to finish what they have to say (the ambush listener).**

- **Acting distracted by something or someone that is not part of the conversation.**

- **Ignoring the speaker.**

- **One-upping the speaker with your examples.**

## Your Lips Say No, But Your Eyes Say Yes

The words flowing from your lips may actually say less than the way your arms are folded. According to Stanford professor emeritus Dr. Albert Mehrabian, 55 percent of the impact of what we say comes from our body language. Body language is defined as nonverbal, and mostly unconscious, communication through use of gestures, postures, and facial expressions. To the trained eye, it can reveal the thoughts of anyone and everyone, as well as their current emotional condition, without saying a word.

Examples of this can be seen in every aspect of business; a woman who is conscious of having gained weight about her thighs will smooth her pants or dress down before she gets up to present, and a customer who wants to be left alone keeps his head down and doesn't make eye contact with anyone. The average woman has over 14 areas of her brain dedicated to communication, whereas the average man will only have between four and six. So does this mean that women can communicate better than men? No, not at all; it does, however, mean that the majority of men will have to consciously try to read a person's body language, whereas most women will automatically do it subconsciously. In the field of customer hospitality, it is important to understand people's gestures. These more often than not indicate whether or not they want help. It will also help you gain a balanced view of their true feelings toward your products or services.

One of the most common mistakes a sales associate makes is to interpret individual gestures in isolation of other gestures. Sometimes people have behaviors that are habitual and don't convey the proper meaning. It sends a mixed message—you need to look at all the gestures, not just one. Often described as the windows to the soul, the eyes can give us great insight into the true thoughts and feelings of a person in any situation. When someone is feeling positive, when they like a product or service, and when they hear something that they agree with, their pupils will dilate. When someone is feeling negative, when they're annoyed, or when they hear something they don't believe, their pupils will contract. Dilating and contracting pupils are known as "microgestures"—they cannot be consciously controlled and often go unnoticed by the untrained eye.

Making lots of eye contact is a way to show interest and respect. The more eye contact a customer makes with you, the more they like and trust you. The more you look into a customer's eyes while you talk to them, the more credible you seem. It is important to remember that making too much eye contact early on in a relationship can sometimes make people feel pressured and insecure. If you are trying to make a good impression on someone, build up a slight rapport first, and then gradually increase the amount of eye contact you give them.

Smiles are often big indicators of whether or not a customer wants you to talk to them. Most people, however, don't realize is that there are different types of smiles, and that each type of smile can mean something completely different. Therefore, when someone is smiling at you, it isn't always a signal to make your move and go talk to them. Not all smiles are positive. A tight-lipped smile, for instance, is spotted frequently in the return department. The lips are stretched across the face forming a straight line, and the teeth are not visible. The tight-lipped smile is often used by someone who is hiding something that they don't want to share with you. *"Yeah, I know this is dirty and the tags have been cut off, but I never wore it, I swear."*

Along with eyes and smiles, hand gestures are another important area of body language to study. There are two basic rules you have to remember when looking at hand gestures: Open palms (when you can see the palms of someone's hands) suggests openness, honesty, and a liking; while closed palms (when you can see the back of someone's hands) suggests that they may be hiding something, are closed to your ideas, or are feeling like they are in authority.

When people apologize, they may say something like "I'm sorry" coupled with presenting their two open palms. The open-palmed gesture is like saying "I'm comfortable around you, I trust you, I am being honest, and I have nothing to hide." If you see a customer or coworker making open-palmed gestures at you, take this to heart and read their other gestures to confirm how they are feeling.

Closed-palm gestures are used frequently too. For example when it's 85 degrees outside and an associate tells you they don't feel well and want to go home, look at their hands. If they're hiding them behind their back or digging to China in their pockets, you can bet the only fever they have is spring fever. Again it is important to bear in mind that hands in pockets may also simply mean that the person is cold, or something else, but if it is a warm day outside, this is probably not the case. Remember to read all gestures in groups and in context.

Just like with palm gestures, when a customer wants to talk to you, they will adopt an open-body position. An open-body position can be spotted by looking at the angle of their body relative to yours. The closer two people are emotionally, the closer they will stand, sit, or lie next to each other. Unless you work in a massage parlor or out of the back of a van, you don't need to violate a customer's personal space. Imagine a bubble around each and every person. This bubble encompasses the person and a small surrounding area. To that person, everything inside that bubble is "theirs," and is known as their personal space. The size of this personal space varies a little from person to person but doesn't differ to a great degree. The average is two to three feet.

Not everyone likes to be touched, but if you're one of those touchy-feely people who can't keep your hands to yourself, touch a customer or coworker on the elbow. Elbows are acceptable because they're far away from the intimate parts of the body. Touch a customer anywhere above or below the elbow and you may be punched in the stomach or given a phone number, depending on the circumstance.

In body language, the arms are known as barriers that are put up to protect a person from harm. Arm gestures are typically used when a person is lacking in self-confidence, feels threatened, or just doesn't want to hear what you are currently saying. Arm gestures don't definitively mean "I don't want you to approach me." However, they do indicate when a person is having negative feelings toward you. When someone is using repetitive negative arm gestures, coupled with crossed legs or ankles, you'll know it's time to leave them alone and let them look around by themselves. Both arms are folded across the chest—this is a universal signal. Its meaning is clear: "I don't agree with what you are saying, I am uncertain, I don't like this situation."

Although body language is universal in its meanings, it really is very easy to get confused or mixed up when reading people's body language. The more you practice reading body language correctly, the easier it will become. Always remember to read gestures in groups, and always remember to take into account the environment around the person you are reading.

### How'd I Do? What Did You Think?

Feedback isn't just something you hear at a Rolling Stones concert. It is also an important aspect of communication. Your staff and customers need to have feedback from you on a regular basis, and not just the good stuff either. Those kind words are nice to hear, but they are not nearly as helpful as corrective feedback. Notice we said *corrective* feedback. Corrective feedback needs to involve specific information. It should also be supportive and encourage people to look for more ways to improve. In order to create an environment of effective communication between associates and customers, it is necessary to build a relationship of trust. Help them perfect their talents and find their genius.

Many of the problems that occur in the field of customer hospitality are the direct result of people failing to communicate properly. Communication is nothing more than the exchange and flow of information and ideas from one person to another. Poor communication leads to confusion and can cause your associates or worse, a customer, to walk out of your establishment and never return. Effective communication occurs only if the receiver understands the exact information or idea that the sender intended to transmit. So when you tell your associate to go into the storeroom and get that thingamajig off the top shelf, don't be too surprised if they look at you like you're crazy. The same is true with your customers; they don't want to talk to a person who stumbles and bumbles over every word. Could you imagine trying to buy a car seat for your firstborn from a person who can't make it through a sentence without saying the work "like" or "um" ten thousand times?

Studying the communication process is important because you coach, coordinate, counsel, evaluate, and supervise through this process. It is the chain of understanding that integrates the members of an organization from top to bottom, bottom to top, and side to side as well as instills a sense of confidence for your customers.

# Action Steps

1.  Shadow your associates and see how they communicate with customers.

2.  Set up role-playing scenarios in which your associates have to communicate with customers in different situations—i.e., a customer complaint, phone call, greeting—and then ask for feedback from the other staff members.

# Chapter 8

## Love You, Want You, Need You

In the area of customer hospitality, there is nothing truer than the age-old adage that hindsight is 20/20. As companies, we invest enormous amounts of money and energy testing and measuring our market and customers, trying to figure out what they want, when really it's a simple question of just asking them and listening to what they want. Why don't they spend their money with us? What makes them do business with our competitors? This is why it is so vitally important to find out who your customers are and what they want. Oh, by the way, this process isn't just for new entities either. It is equally important for existing businesses to keep track of this as well.

Your target audience or market is defined as the people who are most likely to find value in and then purchase what you're selling. Wow! Once you know who you're after and you get them to purchase from you on a regular basis, then you have turned your target audience or market into repeat business. In order to do that, you must tap into your target market's subconscious mind and tug at their heartstrings because people buy on emotion (80 percent emotion, 20 percent logic). Throughout our career with Your Success Coach, we've heard many a business person, when asked about their customers, reply, "Everyone. Everyone needs my service or product." While a business owner might think this is true, it rarely is. There are always some people who care nothing about your product. Let's face it; if you're selling canoes, you probably aren't going to sell too many to people who hate the water or better yet, live in a desert. You're not going to sell coffee to someone who likes tea—you get the idea. There are always some people who desperately want your product and everyone else falls somewhere in between. No matter what your product or service is, there are those who are more likely to need it more than others.

Your job as a marketer is to seduce them into buying without them knowing it. Ingredients for success in this area include being truly unique, understanding their point of view, being exciting to their emotions, having something that they absolutely must share with their friends, and something that can't be copied easily. For example, think about Starbucks. They have a loyal following of people due to their unique brand of coffees, teas, and other consumables. Their logo is one of the most recognizable out there. They are quick and efficient. The customers feel a sense of pride when they walk out with that cup of java or chai. They flaunt it on top of their desk—that they just paid $5 for a cup of coffee.

Remember that customer hospitality and building long-lasting relationships isn't about attracting any Joe Blow off the street; it is about attracting the most lucrative customer possible for the highest return on dollars spent. Business owners must keep this idea front and center. So, before you set up shop, you've got to know exactly who you're aiming for. For example, in one year, Ford Motor Company spent $26 million to produce 30-second commercials to play during the first season of *American Idol*, and they had a drop in sales for that year. The lifetime value of a customer is priceless. Here's an example: Let's say the average transaction amount for a customer is $1,000 a month. Multiplying that by 12 months equals $12,000 per year. Let's say the customer stays loyal for ten years, which means $120,000 of lifetime value. You do the math.

How many customers do you have a month, what's their average transaction amount, and how long will they remain loyal? Failure to identify and connect with your customers can potentially cost you hundreds of thousands in wasted dollars. Over half of the success of your business is a function of how well you've identified this specified group of people. When researching your customers, keep in mind that your market may be an entire segment, a niche within that segment, or a select few within a niche. If, for instance, you want to market skateboards, do you select the corporate office, franchisees, or store managers? Knowing your customer base will also enable you to offer your product in a way that your prospect will relate to. You may have the best product or service in the world, but if you don't get it in front of the correct people and establish a relationship, your products are destined for the recycling bin.

When your company discusses marketing strategies for a new product or service, you should first take time to consider who will get the most benefit from what you are offering. It is important to be as specific as possible. For example, young men are a broad category. Are you referring to men between the ages of 18 and 25? Currently enrolled in college? Graduated from college? Entered the workforce right after high school? Married? Single? This list goes on and on.

Let's take an example of a waterproof backpack. What do you think your return on investment would be if you marketed to a general customer base of young men? Probably marginal at best, because only a certain segment of them use backpacks. Now, let's say you narrow down your audience to young men enrolled in college or trade schools between the ages of 17 and 22 in the Pacific Northwest. Do you think your results would be better? Of course, because you've specifically defined prospects who have a need for your product and are also historically heavy purchasers of similar items from other companies. A more detailed description of potential customers gives a much clearer picture of who your business and product is meant to connect with. Here's an important statistic to keep in mind: eight out of ten products launched in the United States each year are destined to fail. So be sure you know what you're making and who you're making it for.

Of course, if you have an existing business, the best source of information about who will be interested in your product or services is your existing customer base. Spend some time defining who your customers are: what they do; where they live; their age, sex, interests. Then take that information and look at the sales associated with those individuals who are your best customers. Who among them brings in the most profit for you? It is not unusual for a business to be surprised by these results, as your most common (or "average") customer may not be your most profitable.

Let's assume you own a bakery, and your average customer is a woman about 35 years old with children at home. This customer visits your business twice a week and spends an average of $30 each visit. But remember, this isn't about average—it's about profit. Now you look at your data and realize your most profitable customers are women in their early 60s who visit your establishment once a week and spend an average of $75. Doesn't it make much more sense to attract more 60-year-old customers? By establishing a relationship with these customers rather than attracting more "average" customers, you make more profit; and since this customer actually visits your store less often, you will save money on other expenses like staff. Now those are customers worth targeting!

When you are trying to categorize the customers you want to target, there are many various differentiations possible, but they generally fall into two broad categories:

- **Demographics.**

- **Psychographics.**

Demographics are specific definable traits that customers share. These include age, gender, occupation, home value, and many other specific traits. Psychographics refers to the attitudes and beliefs held by a particular person or group of people. These include things such as a need for status, early adoption of technology, or affinity for the arts. You must look at both broad categories, because each set of traits has an impact on buying behavior and your packaging method, communication, and price. Obviously the products you're marketing have a tremendous impact on which target audience you want to reach, but the following suggestions should always be considered:

**Sex.** What percentage is male and female? Fifty-fifty is too simple and usually not correct. Depending on location and other factors like age, the male-female ratio may be skewed in one direction or another. Also, the people using your product will almost always be more of one sex than the other. When determining this, don't necessarily worry about who will use your end product or service, but who makes the decision on what business to frequent. For example, in the past women may have made the vast majority of buying decisions for personal products, furniture, and services such carpet cleaning. But today, they are a major deciding factor for electronics, outdoor equipment, and automobiles. The roles of men and women in society are changing and you need to be aware of the evolution.

**Age.** Determining the best age range of potential customers gives you the ability to create a mental image of them. A word of caution: don't discriminate; just because someone is 65 doesn't mean they sit in a rocker on their front porch. As the baby boomer population ages, they refuse to go into old age quietly, and so many have maintained a much more youthful lifestyle. It is equally a mistake to assume every 25-year-old has aspirations of being in the corporate world, or fits the stereotypical mold of what we deem appropriate patterns for this age group. The younger generations value things such as time off and social networks much more than their predecessors did. Don't let your preexisting beliefs about age override the data.

**Marital status.** Keep in mind this is no longer just two categories—married or single. Consider if they're divorced, separated, or widowed as well. There are also long-term unmarried relationships and same-sex relationships. Another category these days is what we call frequent fliers—those who have been married three or more times.

**Occupation.** What does your customer base do for a living? Are they blue-collar factory workers or CEOs and high-level management? Also consider the transient nature of their occupation. Are they in a job that requires frequent relocation or where they change titles and positions every few years? Rare is the person who stays in any job longer than seven years, so make sure you know where your customers fit. Generations X and Y coming into the workforce will have at least ten career and job changes during their lifetime.

**Income.** How much do they make? By determining their income range, you will be able to pick those customers most likely to buy—but that doesn't mean aiming for the wealthiest. The wealthy may not see a need for your product, so here again, knowing your most profitable customer is essential. Your most profitable customer may be one who earns $100,000 per year rather than one who brings home $250,000. It's also important to determine their spending habits. Is money no issue, or do they live frugally and watch every dollar they spend? This information is essential because it helps you to determine what type of offer might appeal the most. Of even greater importance is a consumer's discretionary spending ability. Regardless of their income, if they are buried in mortgages and consumer debt, the amount left to purchase your product or service may still be very limited. Companies like Echelon offer a service called the discretionary spending index that can be applied to list selects.

**Geographic region.** The importance of this category is determined by the product or service you are selling. If you are a specialty coffee store, most of your business will come from those who live or work within a few blocks or typically within three miles of your location. If you are selling high-end backpacks, then your market may be across the northwest United States and Canada. If you are located in a largely rural area, you deal with those who may drive as far as 100 miles to do business with you. All of these issues will dictate how you most effectively communicate with your customers. However, most neighborhood businesses will find that the overwhelming majority of their sales come from consumers who live no more than ten miles or ten minutes from their front door.

Once you determine your customer base, you've taken the first step to establishing a relationship. Now you need to determine the best technique to build the relationship. Take a look at your customer hospitality. How many complaints do you receive? How many of your customers are first-time or repeat ones? How often do you take a long hard look at yourself and your company? Are your employees treating each one with respect and dignity? Defining your target audience can only take you so far. What happens once you've defined your customer base and you still don't have any business? You can't blame the customers instead of your product or service. More often than not, we are driven to look at what was wrong with our customers because it is a way of being self-protective, as in, "If I know what is wrong with them, I can market to a different client base or find a new product."

Oddly enough, customer relationships just don't work like that. Knowing what was wrong with your customers will not fix anything, because there isn't anything to fix. There is only one way to avoid that and it is by looking at how *you* treat your customers. In a nutshell, the question isn't "What was wrong with them?" The vital questions are "What's wrong with me and my team?" and "How do we correct our actions?" If you are feeling a little squirmy and uncomfortable right now as you read those words, just know you have some thinking to do. You have to look inward for the opportunities and situations, not outward.

The foundation of good communication with your customers is through the development of trusting relationships. You may have a slew of satisfied customers today, but one smug employee comment later, they're out the door and gone forever. So you see, it is important to form not only a good relationship with your customers but one with your employees as well, especially the ones on the front line. One common theme we've seen with Your Success Coach is that one of the most prevalent areas companies neglect is creating an emotional bond between its employees and customers.

By bond we don't mean two hearts beating as one or a Romeo and Juliet scenario. The last thing we want is for you to walk in one morning and find an employee holding a picture of her favorite customer while smearing lipstick on her face. Can you say creepy!! What we're referring to is customer engagement. This goes beyond a single interaction; instead, engagement is defined by enduring behaviors and attitudes that create a connection. An organization's revenue can skyrocket through strong customer relationships.

Engagement is one of the most powerful opportunities for growth available to businesses today. The commoditization of markets, the high amount of competition, the ease of shopping, and the speed at which customers switch their loyalties today makes engagement imperative to stay competitive. In the simplest of terms, engaged employees create engaged customers, thus creating repeat business. With this practice, you can expect

- **Loyalty from both sides of the counter.**

- **Positive word-of-mouth marketing (W.O.M.M.).**

- **Higher profit margin because customers are willing to pay a premium for not only the product but the customer hospitality as well.**

- **Reduced turnover and training costs, which also leads to a better bottom line.**

## You Guys are the Best; I'll Never Go Anywhere Else Again

Engagement provides and an opportunity to gain a competitive advantage with some of the biggest assets any business has—its employees and customers. Have you ever had someone in your life who would go the nth degree for you? If you asked them to walk through hell to get you a glass of water, they'd ask if you wanted ice. No matter what the situation was, they were always at your side. Well, that is what you want from your customers. If you're a mom-and-pop shop next door to Mega Value Mart, you want them to park in their lot and walk over to your store. Engaged customers are more than satisfied and more than loyal; they go out of their way to show their association with your company. They become an active promoter of your business, and support you during good and bad times. In the end, they make you more money. Our goal in customer hospitality is to have engaged customers who are passionate about our products and services and agree with the purpose and direction of our business.

So, now that we have an understanding of the tremendous benefits of engaged customers, some of you may be wondering, okay, Leanne and Victoria, how do we *actually* engage them? Throughout the last thirty years of our experience, we've learned that the best method to engage customers is to give them above and beyond what their expectations are with your company. The "Golden Rule" says to treat others how *you* would want to be treated. The "Platinum Rule" says treat others how *they* would want to be treated. Our "Diamond Rule™" says go above and beyond what anyone's expectations could possibly be. Excite and delight them. Don't just open the door for them as they leave; carry their bags to the car and help them load their trunk. Take the product out of the packaging and show them how it works instead of reading the instructions to them. Or here's one that most companies wouldn't even think about doing; if you don't have a product, call around to your competitors and help your customer find what they're looking for. Most employees won't do this because it goes against their instincts. Give another company our business? No way. They'll never come back. Wrong; they'll remember the fabulous customer hospitality they received and will come back time and time again. Actions speak louder than words and your customers will remember them *and* you.

From the point of view of your customers, they begin to form a strong emotional bond or attachment each time they receive beneficial or enjoyable hospitality. These types of positive experiences make customers feel valued and important to the business, which evolves into confidence. As your customers become more confident in their customer-company relationship, additional helpful experiences stimulate an even stronger bond or attachment toward your company and create a never-ending cycle of repeat business.

Over time, customer hospitality engenders trust with its customers. According to recent research by the Economist Intelligence Unit, companies across the world report that the number one factor that influences the purchase decisions of customers is trust. Once trust is established, customers relate to the vision and direction of the company. They gain a sense of protection and security and consequently develop a strong connection with the company. Engagement implies trust, and you can't have authentic engagement in the absence of a trusting relationship. Customers may forgive honest mistakes, but they will never forgive dishonesty.

Understanding who your customers are, why they want to do business with you, and why they are emotionally engaged with you, is a critical ingredient in building relationships. Price is no longer a consideration for customers when they buy products or services. They're willing to overlook cost in exchange for quality, customer hospitality, and a sense of belonging. If any of these elements are overlooked, customers feel slighted. But if these elements exceed expectations, your customers feel rewarded. We've learned that all of these items *must* be better than expended to maintain a satisfactory customer relationship over time. The theme song to *Cheers* comes to mind here; we all want to spend our money where everybody knows our name.

# Action Steps

1.  If you haven't determined your target market, do so. If you have, revisit it. Has your target audience evolved? Do your products or service still fit in with your current customer base?

2.  Determine whether or not your customers are emotionally engaged. If so, how do you strengthen the bond? If not, how do you create the bond?

3.  Look at ways to develop a strong relationship with your customers. Do you need to hire more staff, move them to different areas of your company, or initiate training?

# Chapter 9

Have you ever found yourself bleary-eyed, strung out from too much coffee, and frantic while making every possible attempt to cram a mandatory eight-hour sexual harassment refresher course into the last hour of the day? You know the feeling; you're sitting at your desk playing solitaire and then suddenly a sense of panic sets in. Your stomach churns, palms sweat, and you collect yourself as best you can, lean over the cubicle, and whisper, "Our continuing education courses are due tomorrow, right?" Only you already know the answer is today, now, right now. You look at your watch: 3:49, an hour and ten minutes left in the day. The panic prayer begins. "Oh God, if you let me finish this today, I'll go to church every Sunday … and Wednesday … OK, every day of the week. I'll help children, feed the homeless, take in stray pets, even cats, just please, please let me finish this module."

You had 90 days, so what was your reasoning for waiting until the last minute? Or have you ever wanted to kick yourself for placing that project your manager told you about at the beginning of the quarter to the side, and waiting until the eleventh hour so you ended up throwing together 20 pages of "crap" just to get the report in on time? Or how about the time your computer crashed the day before you were going to clean out your inbox and you lost the email with your largest customer's contact information?

If you can relate to any of these behaviors, don't feel too bad; you are like most people. We all have the ability to put off until tomorrow what we know we should be working on today. It's human nature. The problem arises whenever this ineffective use of our time interferes with or prevents us from getting our job done. Are there several different tasks you wish you could accomplish at your job—anything from something as grand as finishing your year-end workload to as minuscule as cleaning off your desk? But perhaps you believe there is never enough time in the workday.

What is the reasoning behind the fact that some of us always appear to have the time to accomplish all of our to-do list while others crumble due to the constant demands and pressures and responsibilities of their job? Do those people have more time than the rest of us? Truthfully, we all have the same amount of time, 24 hours in a day. It's finite and you can't, no matter how many black candles you light or how much magic dust you sprinkle, conjure up any more. The difference lies in how we organize our time in a day, take personal responsibility for our actions, and hold ourselves accountable for a planned and structured day. Organizing your schedule is not a difficult task at all; in fact, time management is really more about managing activities and their outcomes. Let's take the example of Facebook, Twitter, and personal email. Do you think you're paid to yap with your friends all day? No, you were hired to do a specific job. You wouldn't walk into a convenience store and steal a candy bar, would you? No, of course not; common sense dictates that's wrong. Well, the same is true with using your time at work to find out the latest gossip and plan your social life.

## In a Minute

The majority of people do not get any work done because they are procrastinators. Basically, a procrastinator is someone who puts off the work that they are supposed to do for a later time. Why do today what you can do tomorrow? Because you can lose your job, that's why. What if your job was to inspect a load of tapioca pudding before it shipped out to several elderly care facilities, but you just didn't feel like sorting through a sea of cans that afternoon? You rationalize and think to yourself, "I'll get to it in a minute." Three hours later, the truck left the shipping yard without an inspection. Let's take it a step further: the tapioca was tainted and because of you, grandmas and grandpas across the country had to have their diapers changed every hour for two days.

Now that you understand how bad procrastination can be, do you ever find yourself placing tasks on the back burner? In our time and activity management trainings, procrastination is one of the biggest problems we see. An important point we'd like to note is that if you procrastinate in one aspect of your life, you more than likely procrastinate in all areas. So if you put off items in your personal life, the same is true with your job. Procrastination doesn't discriminate; everyone from CEOs to frontline employees deals with this problem.

The following questions are a good guideline to help you determine whether or not you procrastinate:

- **Have you ever told yourself that if you ignore an assignment from your manager, maybe it will go away?**

- **Have you ever told yourself, "I'll say hello to those customers as soon as they walk past my counter"?**

- **Have you ever replaced high-importance activities by low-importance activities?**

- **Have you ever done something else "very important" like checking your inbox to avoid working on a presentation?**

- **Have you ever only worked on the portion of the job you enjoyed or were good at and ignored the part you had didn't like or had difficulties with?**

How many questions did you answer yes to? One, two, or maybe even all of them? We procrastinate for many reasons. We may be overwhelmed by too much work, and we know that we can't get them all done. Or we don't think that we have the skills or aren't clear about what is expected. Another reason people procrastinate is because they feel the job is too time-consuming. They stop before they ever start! Inventory is a prime example of this. It has to be done, but it is such a pain in the rear that everyone avoids it. Basically, the reasons don't matter. All that does matter is that you're able to realize why you're doing so and what the consequences are.

If you postpone doing a certain activity, it is going to affect you later. Let's go back to the inventory example. It has to be done, no bones about it. If businesses don't have an accurate account of their inventory, they don't know how much to order, don't have an accurate representation of the products that sell and the ones that don't, or aren't able to pay the correct amount of taxes. As a result this can cost you lost sales and, worse still, a potential audit.

With all of the detrimental effects of procrastination, the question is, then, why do we postpone work? You see, procrastinators constantly postpone important, frustrating, or difficult work, and they convince themselves that some other work is more important. A huge misconception is that procrastinators waste time. What we've found is just the opposite. They in fact are actually quite busy avoiding the work they need to complete by looking for other activities. Procrastinators convince themselves that they must postpone the current job at hand to do a more "important" task.

The best method to overcome procrastinating is to just do it. Dig your heels in and plow through the chore at hand. We wish we could give you some magical formula or some fairy dust to sprinkle and make procrastination go away, but the truth is there is no such thing. As an employer, you may be thinking to yourself, "Right, tell that to my employees." The key to helping your employees to overcome procrastination is to empower them. If you're too strict and always tell your employees exactly what is to be done, when it is to be done, and how it is to be done, you don't allow them to develop the ability to work on their own. They aren't able to develop the confidence to decide what to do.

Let the members of your team learn to do things by themselves. Give them the freedom to choose to accomplish the job on time or to postpone it. Whenever they do follow through and finish on time, reward them. A word of praise many times means more than money. Why? Because money is fleeting and a compliment or congratulations stay in a person's mind. Encourage staff members to make the correct choices, give them the freedom to act based on their instincts rather than just on your orders, and show them gratitude. This practice eliminates procrastination and makes your staff more productive.

## I Think I Can, I Think I Can

We're sure most of you have uttered the words at some point in your career, or life for that matter: "There is just not enough time in the day." Too much to do, too little time—or time poverty— we simply do not have enough time to fulfill our responsibilities. The next time you belt out these words, take a moment and ask yourself, "What's stopping me from using my time wisely?" Now more than ever, there is increasing demand for time, activity, and project management training, primarily because many companies have downsized *and* expect more from their remaining employees. This is a double-edged sword. While the increased productivity expands the company's bottom line, the greater demands on employees can leave many feeling overwhelmed and less than enthusiastic about going to work each day. Time is a nonrenewable resource, and we need to learn to manage it effectively. Basically, time and activity management is our ability to prioritize, follow a schedule, and accomplish our task at hand. Time and activity management is much more about choices and decisions than compiling to-do lists. It's planning and preparing in advance—in an organized fashion—how to accomplish your goals in a day, week, month, year, and decade.

All of the lists, calendars, and electronic organizational devices don't mean squat if you fail to understand this one important fact. To meet deadlines and minimize distractions at work, you have to first accept that you are responsible for how you spend your time, and accountable for your actions. Time and activity management can help you manage the events at work much better and reduce your stress, but only if you're willing to take responsibility for your decisions. In the workplace, there are always going to be choices. Do you call your spouse instead of dust the shelves? Check your email rather than prepare for the staff meeting?

Accepting responsibility for your time and activities means you have to realize that it is your choice whether or not you manage your time effectively. Situations, events, circumstances, coworkers, and even management can, at times, distract us and cause us to think, "If they would just leave me alone, I could get this job done. " Did it ever occur to you that maybe the people in the office don't realize they're wasting your time? Again, this is where responsibility comes into play. By denying this fact, we blame others or the circumstances surrounding our situation. You alone are responsible for how you use your time. No one in this world is more responsible than you for protecting your time. Not your supervisor. Not your coworkers. Not even your customers. Just you.

Our attitude drives our behavior, and this is certainly the case with time and activity management. Are you one of those who believes there is just not enough time in the day? Hit the snooze button several times because you can't bear the thought of how much you have to do? Your attitude toward time determines your stress level and how you manage your actions. Think about a kid on a long car ride. "Are we there yet? Are we there yet?" Their impatience makes the trip seem 10,000 times longer. Are you tense because you're under the gun to finish a huge project by the end of the week? The amount of stress you're under determines your productivity. How effective are you when you feel stress? Does your attitude add value or stress to your day? How about to your customers, employees, and employer?

When you consider we all have the same amount of time given to us every day, have you ever stopped to wonder why so many people are able to do so much—and others say they could do so many things if only they had the time? The difference between the two is

- **Their willingness to accept responsibility.**

- **Their attitude toward time.**

- **Holding themselves accountable to get it done.**

Remember, the biggest challenge to time and activity management isn't the hours on the clock but the space between your ears.

## Deviate from Distractions

How many times have you ever started a project, determined to finish, only to find yourself wondering at the end of the day why you didn't finish? In the beginning, you're most productive, but as the day progresses, less and less is completed. What is the reason for this? The main reason for this is that initially when you begin an activity, distractions are at a minimum because your energy and motivation are high. As the day progresses, the phone rings, you get involved with gossip at the water cooler, emails, temptations from other coworkers, and anything else you can imagine. Distractions are not just something that you can avoid like a bump in the road; they seek you out. These interruptions evolve as well. Let's say you just want to check one email. You sit down at the computer after promising yourself to "make it quick." Before you know it, you've spent three hours surfing your mail and two hours answering it. You've spent the whole day doing something that was only supposed to take a few minutes. We don't think of emails as distractions. Ordinarily we would never sit in front of the TV for an entire day without feeling at least a small bit of guilt. Why? Because we know this isn't work. But checking email feels like work, so we don't realize that we're wasting our day away. The problem is a hard one to solve because email increasingly is used to communicate. If, for example, you smoke, you can solve that problem by stopping. But you can't alienate yourself from your business contacts.

We need to be more organized and meet our deadlines by working efficiently. The first necessary step in eliminating interruptions and managing your time is to prioritize. Get a notebook, piece of paper, blank document on your computer—any manner of recording you prefer—and start writing down your priorities. You need this list to be able to see what is in the way of your job. What unimportant activities or thoughts are taking up your time and energy? Once you have your list in place, the items on the list become your guiding priorities. For instance, if you're tempted to blow off work and hang out with your buddies, is this worth your time based upon your priorities? If you have rent and a family to take care of, probably not. Do not let anyone pressure you to do something that takes your time and energy away from your priorities. Write down and track every distraction and interruption that gets in the way of your priorities. Once you've done that, put a plan in place to get rid of them and hold yourself accountable to it.

Today more than ever, Generation Y employees face distractions. Technological advances such as email, instant messaging, and cell phones have forced us into a society that expects instant response, which consequently leads to more and more distractions. So what are these weapons of mass distraction that prevent employees and even employers from staying focused?

**The Cell Phone.** This revolutionary communication device has become a major distraction because, for some reason, people just can't seem to keep their hands off of them. Text messaging, games, and annoying ringtones. After all, it's hard to imagine that your job is more interesting than what you friends and coworkers have to say, right? Even if you are the best at doing a multitude of tasks, you still aren't able to give your full attention to your customers and your cell phone at the same time.

**Instant Messenger.** IM is an especially insidious distraction because it interrupts you while you work on your computer. You may be fully engrossed in completing an order for a customer, but when your wife IMs you, asking you to pick up a gallon of milk on the way home, your concentration is gone. IM is just as bad as text messaging.

**Social Networking Sites.** These sites can take you away from your work. We know; there have been many hours spent in front of the computer with these sites. What sounds better, helping a customer or checking your friend's status? Customers don't stand a chance against these sites.

So with so many fun ways to avoid your work, how can you be expected to pay attention? Learning how to pay attention in such a technologically rich environment is not an easy task, even for the best employees. But the thing is, if you're going to succeed, you need to learn how to resist temptation and pay attention to your customers. The majority of employees spend their days doing a good deal of "stuff" that doesn't really make an impact. We need to take a hard look periodically at how we spend our time and purge tasks that are no longer necessary, and at the same time, have the ability and willingness to adapt to the constantly changing work demands. Listed below are a few questions to ask yourself when confronted with distractions.

• **Is this a priority?**

• **Can this be rescheduled for a different time?**

• **How can this be done in the most efficient manner possible?**

• **Can this be delegated to another staff member and what can I do to help them get it done?**

In the last section we discussed the detriments of procrastination. Well, procrastination is fueled by distractions. The majority of us find it uncomfortable to sit idle when we have a job to do, so we tend to avoid work by doing something else. The best technique to rid yourself of the tendency to procrastinate is to eliminate distractions. At a seminar in the Bell Communications Research Colloquia Series, Dr. Richard W. Hamming, a professor at the

Naval Postgraduate School in Monterey, California, and a retired Bell Labs scientist, presented a speech titled "You and Your Research" regarding his research on the question "Why do so few scientists make significant contributions, and why are so many forgotten in the long run?" While working at Bell Labs, Hamming started asking such questions about productivity. He suggests that you ask yourself three questions:

- **What are the most important problems in your field?**

- **Are you working on one of them?**

- **Why not?**

Hamming used to spend a portion of his day asking people these questions. He knew that this didn't make him popular, but he also realized that anyone ambitious should be willing to ask themselves these questions. When lack of time and distractions are a problem, your first consideration should be the "big picture." Everyone should try to prioritize their life, regardless of whether it is professional or personal. Time is equal for everybody; whether you are a big shot or just a small entrepreneur, you get the same 24 hours.

Just as Hamming asked his employees these questions, we need to do the same. Effective time and activity management heavily relies on the questions we consistently ask ourselves on a daily basis. We should always be focusing our mind on time-saving thoughts that move us away from busyness and into productivity. These types of questions will help us focus on areas that will make us more productive and save us time to do the things that bring a greater sense of fulfillment and satisfaction.

# Action Steps

1. Take note of how many of your associates use cell phones and other personal items during work hours. Is this interfering with customer hospitality?

2. Make a list of items associates can't have on the sales floor such as cell phones and iPods.

3. During an employee evaluation, ask if there is any task that they are having trouble completing. Work together to find out why and how they can accomplish the job as well as come up with solutions to prevent the situation from happening again.

# Chapter 10

They May Be Jerks, But They're Still Right

This applies in all our working relationships. When we think about workplace conflict, we tend to think about relationships with the boss, or with troublesome peers. However, when we, at Your Success Coach, talk to our clients, one of the areas of conflict that they would like to get more from is their relationships with their clients. Client relationships exhibit many of the classic characteristics of conflict: both parties want the best value from the relationship, but they are working from different information and they generally have limited communication. One might, then, assume that any conflicts will be competitive, negative experiences. In some situations this will certainly be true: if an organization has a short-term, transactional relationship with its customers, it need not worry too much about what to do when the customer is unhappy.

However, many organizations now operate in industries where it's far more expensive and difficult to get a new customer than it is to keep an existing one. In such situations it's worth the investment in considering how best to manage conflict situations. Competing is probably not appropriate with such clients, and ignoring the situation will ultimately mean that you lose the customer. Instead, frontline associates need to adopt other strategies that will enhance the relationship, reaping longer-term rewards through a greater understanding of client needs.

There is also evidence from the other side of this relationship. For clients, when there is a problem, the treatment they receive from their supplier has a significant impact in either direction. If conflict is handled badly, the relationship will certainly be soured, and they may consider taking their business elsewhere. But if the conflict is handled well, the client's belief and loyalty in the company can actually increase through greater trust that their needs are understood and that future problems can also be overcome by working through difficult issues together.

Organizations address this by considering how they train and support frontline associates and middle management. Conflict is rarely comfortable at the time, and staff will need support to deal with the impact of disagreements. The obvious sources for this are their team and their manager, although it's important to balance empathizing with the individual by showing respect for customers because they are customers.

A lack of confidence and skill can be a good excuse for not addressing problems with clients, or even for failing to set their expectations properly around tricky issues such as payment or contracts. Ensuring that everyone has a chance to practice and develop their conflict management skills in a safe environment increases their effectiveness when working with real clients. Training that contains a component on understanding individual differences, such as psychometrics, provides client-facing staff with the insight that makes for lasting behavior change, rather than just a short-term cosmetic impact. In short, share with your staff what the expectations of their job are. Begin there. First, *tell* them what to do. Second, *show* them how to do it. Train and teach them how to be a success on the job. Third, *allow* them to *practice.*

Fourth, *provide feedback*. Let them know how they're doing and let them know what corrections they need to make. Finally, *celebrate* their successes!

It can be tempting to think that this might just apply to call-center staff handling irate calls about customers' broadband, but many organizations are seeking to develop conflict skills in all client-facing employees, from business developers to project managers and engineers, and even partners of professional services firms.

To create good solutions it's essential to seek a range of opinions, gaining input from those with diverse experiences or personalities, and to manage the process of doing so professionally. As with many organizational challenges, conflict is not the problem; badly managed conflict is.

## The Customer Is Always Right

Everyone has heard the phrase "The customer is always right." But have you ever wondered about the origin of this phrase? In the early twentieth century, several retail stores began using this slogan. It is particularly associated with Marshall Field's department store in Chicago. In the UK, Harry Gordon Selfridge, who opened London's Selfridges store in 1909, is credited with championing its use as well. The Wisconsin-born Selfridge worked for Field from 1879 to 1901. Both men were dynamic and creative businessmen and it's highly likely that one of them coined the phrase, although we don't know which.

Of course, these entrepreneurs didn't intend the saying to be taken literally. What they were attempting to do was to make the customer feel special by inculcating into their staff the disposition to behave as if customers were right, even when they weren't. Whether the phrase was coined by Field or Selfridge, it is fair to call it American. What we can't do is credit them with the idea behind it. In 1908 César Ritz (1850–1918), the celebrated French hotelier, was credited with saying *Le client n'a jamais tort*—"The customer is never wrong." That's not the phrase that people now remember, but it can hardly be said to be any different in meaning to "the customer is always right."

This age-old adage is touted by tens of thousands of large and small business owners, customer service representatives, and even customers. As we've said many times throughout this book, without customers you don't have a business, so yes, they are right. For good reason too: *they pay your bills and your salary.* The majority of us, however, have had at least one experience that made us question this. So is the customer always right? Yes, absolutely. Even the obnoxious, the rude, morons, and liars. Conflicts are a part of every working environment. It is virtually impossible to eliminate disagreements altogether (unless you have a bunch of Stepford Wife employees). Some customers are just going to rub you or your employees the wrong way. Their personalities are abrasive, their tempers are quick, and in short, they are jerks. But guess what? None of this matters. Why, you ask? Again, because the customer is always right, no matter how rudely or insensitively they act. We are here to serve our customers and make them happy. Now please don't misunderstand us; there are those extreme cases. In one of our seminars, we had an employee who worked at a major retail chain in the mall tell us that a woman bought a pair of underwear, wore them for a week (eww!), and then tried to return them. In this instance, the customer wasn't only wrong but incredibly gross.

With situations such as the one above, you have to decide if you want the future business of the customer or not. An important point to remember is that even though your goal is to increase your customer hospitality, you don't have to take abusive behavior. You can draw the line at customers lying or shoplifting. In your business, discuss when you no longer want a person as a customer, so everybody in the business knows that the patron who crosses the line is no longer called a customer. Once a person crosses the line you draw, they cease to have the right to be right.

## In the Immortal Words of Donald Trump, You're Fired

In our culture, we reflexively tend to think of the term "conflict" in the negative. When we discuss conflict in the business world, we speak of it (often unwittingly) as a diminishing force on productivity, an ill that only compounds the difficulties of a job, and an element that needs expunging if companies are to achieve their goals. Normally seen as the byproduct of a squeaky wheel rather than a natural derivative of business itself, conflict is a force that causes short-term anxieties, and many view fixing ongoing conflict as synonymous with eliminating it. The primary causes of workplace conflict are seen as personality clashes and egos the size of the fat lady at the circus. Stress, overbearing workloads, and cultural differences also are additional causes.

In addition, anger, hurt, blame, and lost productivity are direct results of conflict—but they don't have to be. At Your Success Coach, we've learned how to manage conflict more effectively, focus on finding solutions and reaching compromises, and keep the lines of communication open and flowing. It's time that is exceptionally well spent. The best technique to manage conflicts is to do just that—manage them. The sooner you handle them, the better it is for your business; otherwise the conflicts give way to negative behavior and lack of team efforts, and as a result, low productivity and loss of income.

The workforce looks much different today than it did 30, 20, or even ten years ago. With the increasing amount of diversity entering the workforce, businesses are certain to face conflicts. Organizational integration, participatory management, and the alignment of management and staff with purpose, visions, and goals are the new "ins" for today's successful companies. The days of the good-old-boy system are over and we can no longer toss back a scotch and soda in the office, shake hands, and forgive and forget. Now, lawyers, activist groups, and Litigious Larry and Lawsuit Lucy circle corporations like vultures, waiting for the slightest bit of tension so they can swoop in and go for the kill. Yes, it's good to have diversity in the workforce, but any time different types of people are placed together, this often results in differences of opinions and you guessed it—conflicts.

What are some of the basic personality types in the workforce? We've seen them all and would like to introduce them to you. As you read through the list, see how many you recognize in your team.

**They Still Live With Their Mother at 40.** These employees are quiet and keep to themselves. They pay little attention to their appearance, and many people think that they are just plain weird. They have little or no social skills but play a valuable role in your business because they are the ones who pay close attention to detail and almost always see a project through to completion by ensuring that any loose ends are tied up.

**The Guidance Counselor.** These employees are warm and approachable. Everyone turns to them for advice. They are great listeners and always willing to lend an ear or shoulder to cry on. The problem with the Guidance Counselors is that they spend too much time helping everyone and not enough time doing their job.

**The Stand-up Comedian.** They are fun to be around and everyone looks to them for a laugh. Stand-Ups use humor as their primary form of communication and always have time to have a chat and crack a joke with colleagues. This can play a vital role in lightening the mood and lifting the morale of other team members.

**The Stoner.** These employees live in a constant haze of "What the *&%@." They are calm, relaxed, and very laid-back. They have the unique ability to remain unflustered when things start going wrong. One problem with Stoners is that they sometimes don't see the urgency in certain jobs. On the flip side, however, they have a calming effect on their coworkers.

**The Cheerleader.** These employees are enthusiastic, optimistic, and motivating. Some Monday mornings you may want to punch them in the face for their perkiness, but for the most part, they are great motivators for the rest of the team. They have a heaping helping of praise and encouragement for anyone and everyone. Cheerleaders lead by example with their "can-do" attitude and see only opportunities.

**The Wet Blanket.** These employees are always looking on the negative side of things. They are the ones who want to beat up the Cheerleader. They tell it like it is. This trait is good in some instances, because they are able to keep other employees from running away with a new idea before considering the potential pitfalls.

**Mr./Ms. Resourceful.** These employees are creative and think outside of the box. They are the MacGyver of the company. They can save the day with just a paper clip and a pair of socks. They are a perfect addition to the team because they can help them get out of a slump or rut. A word of caution, however; Mr. /Ms. Resourceful are great with the ideas but not so much with putting them into action.

We're all faced with conflicts every day. Are they all annoying? Yes. Do they all affect our job performance? No. You need to make this distinction. For example, if you have a coworker who brings a tuna sandwich every day for lunch and leaves it on his desk, making yours smell like a shipyard, ask yourself if it affects your job? No, probably not, so let it go. Besides, look at it this way. As Gloria Estefan says, the rhythm is going to get you, but in this case the unrefrigerated fish is going to get them eventually, too. However, if you're faced with a situation that affects your ability to do your job successfully or impacts your happiness at work, you owe it to yourself to have a conversation about it. Will you allow it to affect you or infect you? There is a huge difference whether the offensive smell affects you, or will *infect* you to cause you to react emotionally, particularly if it's with a person whom you depend upon a lot.

Companies must learn to accept conflict as an inevitable part of their work environment. Research finds that almost 85 percent of employees experience conflict to some degree. Frontline employees are not the only casualties of conflict. Upper and middle management all the way up to the executive offices deals with conflict too. Did you know that U.S. employees spend 2.8 hours per week on average dealing with conflict, equating to approximately $359 billion in paid hours in 2008? The question for management, therefore, is not whether it can be avoided or mitigated; the real concern is how conflict is dealt with. If managed improperly, businesses' productivity, operational effectiveness, and morale take a major hit, not to mention the fear that some pissed-off employee can burst into the establishment with a machine gun underneath their coat. 27 percent of employees have witnessed conflict morph into a personal attack, while 25 percent say that the avoidance of conflict has resulted in sickness or absence from work.

On the other hand, when channeled through the right tools and expertise, conflict can lead to positive outcomes, such as a better understanding of others, improved solutions to problems or challenges, and major innovation. Roughly three-quarters of workers reported positive outcomes that resulted from conflict—results that in all likelihood would not have been produced if conflict was not initiated and managed.

Despite this, however, our most striking—and alarming—finding was that the majority of employees have never received conflict management training. Furthermore, our concern is magnified by the discovery that stress and workload—two factors certain to increase in a dynamic economy—are the second and third most common causes of conflict. Companies, therefore, that choose to ignore conflict management are risking exposure to a myriad of negative consequences that may dramatically diminish bottom-line performance. On the other hand, organizations that implement effective strategies for dealing with conflict will position themselves for tremendous gains in the years to come.

Shocker: badly managed or ignored conflict is expensive to your company. When an employee spends 2.8 hours per week dealing with conflict, this translates to almost 385 million working days spent every year as a result of conflict in the workplace. Managing conflict is a critically important leadership skill. Most management fails to realize the need to address underlying tension before it escalates into damaging conflict. So the question is then, how do we do this? We can't line our employees up every morning and walk the ranks yelling, "Do you have any conflict?" "Drop and give me twenty for every time you talked crap on your coworker!" No matter how much we'd like to, it is just not possible to make our employees run three miles, jog through tires, and climb up walls for petty acts and stupid remarks.

Training is the most effective tool to teach management and staff how to deal with conflict. Less than half (44 percent) of all those questioned have received training in how to manage workplace conflict. With Your Success Coach, we've seen this firsthand. One of the first questions we ask as soon as we walk in the door is about conflict management and communication skills training. Almost always the answer is no. Why? Because people don't want to deal with anything that makes them uncomfortable. Once we've established training programs, the company sees the added value almost immediately. Over 95 percent of our clients who received training say that it made them more comfortable and confident in managing disputes. This is great because it leads to win-win outcomes from conflict.

Given the multitude of personality types present in any workplace, and the range of internal and external pressures that exist, it is no surprise that conflict exists. What triggers conflict at work? Leadership, or lack of it, is also seen as a significant element in generating conflict at work. But the real question is, whose job is it to manage conflict? The entire organization has a role to play in managing conflict, not just human resource departments and line managers.

Disagreements thrive where there is ambiguity: around the boundaries of job roles or functional teams, the relative importance of organizational priorities, or the ownership of resources. So check your business's policies and procedures for clarity and consistency. Don't expect cross-functional relationships to flourish unless there's a clear steer from the top that this is expected, and provide a strong model of being a good internal partner.

Every conflict presents an opportunity for positive change. Nonetheless, it's harder to realize improvements if management doesn't have the skills to manage potentially difficult conversations in a constructive way that permits creativity to flourish. There are many positive aspects to avoiding conflict. We all know that "sleeping on it" can help us calm down and think about what we really want. The trick to success is ensuring that you do not use this calmer mindset as an excuse for not addressing those issues that may worsen if left unresolved. It's easy to think that ignoring conflict will enable you to reach your individual, team, and organizational objectives more quickly, but this is often self-deceit. Keeping plans a secret in case they're opposed, holding decisions in perpetual limbo while more data is gathered, and deferring meetings endlessly in the hope that circumstances will change are all actions likely to trigger conflict of damaging proportions.

Whenever you get to the bottom of any conflict, you will find the same old cause lying in the roots: a lack of communication. Different types of personality clashes and characteristics are another common problem. Unfair handlings, unmerited promotions, lack of opportunities, or any other thing that results in insecurity among employees can also lead to conflicts. If the work expectations or production targets are too hard to achieve, the workers will get frustrated and demotivated. The offspring of that could be bullying, tension, and mass exodus of people. In conclusion, what do you need to do? Learn to communicate effectively and handle conflict effectively with everyone you interact with.

# Action Steps

1. Determine which of your employees fall into the above personality types.

2. Find a way to make them all work together in the best way for your company. For example, don't put the Cheerleader next to the Wet Blanket.

# Chapter 11

## Where the Rubber Meets the Road

What would you do if one day a sales clerk walks into your office and says, "If you'll give me a raise from $18,000 to $20,000 a year and help me pay for my tuition, I'll sign an employment contract guaranteeing that I'll stay here four more years"? The question isn't what would you do, so much as what should you do. We'd tell you to take it and run. As a matter of fact, we'd probably advise you to offer the same kind of deal to your other associates as well. Why? Because the cost of replacing an employee can be in excess of $50,000. A study conducted by the Institute for Research on Labor and Employment evaluating the effects of the U.S. Family Medical Leave Act (FMLA) discovered that "turnover costs for a manager average 150% of salary." These costs are tangible as well as intangible. They include hiring new workers, lost productivity, and product knowledge.

In any company, regardless of the type, there is an outstanding performer who is well-known within their industry. Their passion shines through their work. It's easy to see that they enjoy everything about their job, including the challenges. We like to call these individuals superstar employees. They consistently achieve and exceed their position's responsibilities. These employees fit into your culture and do whatever it takes to get the job done. Fellow employees may go to them for advice and help with job duties because they have the answers and can always be counted on. We rely and depend on them to propel our business to higher levels.

The most important task you'll ever need to do as a business owner is hiring the right people. This may appear more obvious in small, entrepreneurial companies; it is also applicable to larger corporations. Without them, no amount of money can make a company succeed. This is true primarily because superstar employees have the foresight to help your business succeed. Some companies depend entirely on the strength of their employees to perform services, which is the case with many of the companies we work with, while others sell products or manufacture products for sale. For those who depend on product alone, realize this— you still need people to sell and distribute those items. Machines will never replace the ability of people to think, imagine, develop relationships with other people, and create better methods to improve your company's profit margin.

Today, more than any other time in history, we live in a fast-paced, competitive environment. Our world is shrinking more each day. By this we mean what used to require a week's worth of travel can now be accomplished in a matter of minutes through email, Skype, and many other technological advances. With these advantages come disadvantages too, including the demand of new technologies, new competitors, and the increasing desires of consumers for a better product. As a result, recruiting and retaining superstar employees is vital to the success of our companies. Through our experience with the many businesses we've assisted, we've learned several valuable lessons about finding the right people that we will share with you throughout the rest of this chapter.

## Aim Hire

Would you hire a person who overnighted their resume, using their current employer's air bill number and charging them for it? We hope not. Hiring is one of the most crucial skills an owner or manager can have. Many businesses know the importance of recruiting great employees but fail to recognize the need to leave behind the old model of hiring. Hiding behind your comfort zone of outdated models will leave you with a team of lackluster employees and a high turnover rate. Most organizations focus on technical benchmarks such as education, experience, industry knowledge, and recommendations. Please don't misunderstand us; this is indeed valuable information, but they should not, however, become the basis for your decision whether or not to hire someone. Remember that you can always train a person to do a specific job. You can't, however, train an employee to have good character, to be confident and self-assured.

We interviewed a young "lady" a few years ago for a corporate position who could only be described as showing up in, how should we say this; well, let's just say if anyone needed change she had enough ones to handle the entire crowd. You could have driven a motor home through her cleavage. Couple that with the fact that, when we asked her what her top qualifications were, it sounded like she was auditioning for a pep squad. "Perky, bubbly, and fun to be around," while nice, were really not what we were looking for, and this woman was in her mid-20s so you would think she would know better. Had anything other than high-pitched squeals and giggles come out of her mouth we might have listened.

We need to look at the benchmarks that are critical to success or failure. These are hard to define and many times highly debated. From our experience, we've seen that the ability to work in teams, listen attentively, communicate, and have an overall sense of ease with customers is crucial. Oftentimes, we hear clients discuss their frustrations with the amount of time involved in the hiring process. Yes, it is true that interviewing potential employees is time-consuming, but it is an investment that will reap tremendous dividends in the future. Realize that there are few areas of your business more important than having competent people to support you.

In addition to looking at unconventional benchmarks such as self-motivation, intuition is an important force used for guiding your hiring decisions. At one point or another in our lives, whether it is personal or professional, we've all thought to ourselves, "I've got a feeling about this." This is especially true in the interviewing process. A recent survey conducted by The Creative Group found that 46 percent of executives reported that they rely heavily on their intuition during the hiring process. Using your intuition when hiring someone can be very useful. Although being objective should always be a key factor in our decision making, we cannot ignore our true feelings about someone. Feeling compatible with a candidate will help maintain a good working atmosphere.

Use your intuition and good judgment, but also add an organized, diagnostic procedure when it comes to hiring the right people. During the recruiting process, you must figure out exactly what your company needs. To do this, start by listing your top requirements. Also bear in mind that you shouldn't place your primary focus on whether or not the candidate has the exact experience you're looking for. Instead, consider looking for the most desirable traits, such as

- **Problem-solving skills**

- **Time management**

- **Good social skills**

- The ability to think creatively

- What can they do, what will they do, and will they be able to fit into the culture?

## Don't Blame Them If You Can't Train Them

Skills such as persuasiveness, being financially responsible, and ability to work in different areas outside of their actual position are highly positive traits. It is also important to hire someone who is not afraid of working in a team atmosphere. The need to work in a variety of areas within one company or business continues to grow, as does the need to have good social skills. Cross-training has become a vital part of today's workforce. Cross-training is nothing more than training an associate to do a different part of your business's work. In simplistic terms, it is training worker A to do worker B's job while worker B learns to do worker A's job.

In the majority of the companies we work with, for example, we find that only one person is primarily responsible for handling the entity's various financial matters. This concentration of duties in one person is not desirable for accounting. What happens if that *one person* gets sick or has a family emergency and can't come to work that day? Or worse, what if something happens and that *one person* has to take an extended leave? Who's going to pay the bills, write the paychecks, and make the deposits? The scene of a lynch mob carrying bats, throwing rocks, and torching the place comes to mind when employees don't get their paychecks. Instead of fighting off a potential crisis, counter this weakness by training a second person in the specific job duties related to the company's finances.

In regards to customer hospitality, why not make sure that all of your staff is properly trained to operate certain equipment and know about each product or service offered? We went to have a key copied at our local home improvement store and had to wait for the person to come back from lunch because no one else knew how to operate the key-carving machine. To our surprise, this employee's knowledge was questionable at best, and to top it off he was ten minutes late. We asked him how old he was, and just as we thought, he was only seventeen and still in high school. What are the odds of him making a career of this job? Little to none. So why in the world would this store not have anybody else trained to copy keys!!?

Don't blame them if you can't train them. Companies have no right to get frustrated with an employee for not knowing how to do a specific task if they don't take the time to train them in all fields associated with the business. Cross-training has obvious benefits for both managers and staff. It gives management more flexibility to get the job done right and helps to eliminate boredom for the employees by giving them a new set of skills to learn. Having a second person perform the job duties from time to time also provides a method of detecting errors or irregularities created by the person primarily responsible for those duties. Finally, cross-training provides continuity during periods of employee transitions. A good example of the benefits of cross-training involves frontline employees or receptionists. By training other staff members to answer the phone or check out customers, you won't have an empty phone or desk during the lunch hour.

Training your employees to work in several different areas is suitable for almost any type of company. There are obvious exceptions. You wouldn't, for instance, want a doctor who specializes in colonoscopies to conduct eye surgery on you. If so, you'd have a really crappy outlook. Sorry, we couldn't resist. Cross-training can be used in almost any position in almost any industry and benefits both your business and its employees. Select your employees carefully, however, because not all associates are willing to learn a new skill set. Keep in mind, though, that the benefits of cross-training are numerous and definitely worth the effort.

## Where Were You on the Night of the Fifth?

One of the worst examples we've seen in the interview process happened in a group interview with an applicant who took a cell phone call and went outside while we sat waiting for at least 15 minutes. She came back and explained that that was her husband and they were trying to start a landscaping business on the side, and she always had to be available to take calls from customers. Wow. What an idiot. With the incorrect people, your business will suffer and you'll find your doors may not stay open for any significant amount of time. With superstars on your staff, however, you'll catapult ahead of your competition and establish a team dedicated to the success of both you and your company, which is why the interview process is so important.

During the interviews, it is best to include one or two other colleagues. Often, other employees can provide input on issues that you may not pick up on during the various interview stages. Your employees also know your business and will help give you better insight as to which candidate might be better suited for a position. After completing the interview, always be sure to thoroughly discuss each candidate with the other interviewers. You're attempting to get a three-dimensional targeted interview.

The single most important factor in any interview is language. Primarily we are referring to the words that come out of your mouth. Whether it is answering questions, asking questions, or describing the job, these words are critical. There is, however, an additional, nonverbal language, body language, that also has a major influence on the success of an interview. Just as an interviewee will look for meaning in the words you use, they will also interpret much from your mannerisms. These mannerisms will influence the interviewee's impression of you and your company in many ways, including self-confidence, honesty, and level of interest. Here are several elements of body language and a brief discussion of each. Although some of these concepts were discussed in chapter seven in relation to understanding the body language of customers, they also apply to employee interviews.

**Eye contact.** This is the first piece of body language that comes into play in any interview. Looking the interviewee in the eye and maintaining eye contact throughout the interview says that you are an honest employer and treat your staff with respect.

**Mannerisms/gestures.** Most people have and use them, consciously or otherwise. They can have both a positive and a negative impact. Many of us cannot communicate without hand gestures. That is fine, as long as the "talking with your hands" does not become distracting. Some people are naturally fidgety—they just cannot sit still. They squirm in their seat. They constantly cross and uncross their legs or reposition their hands. Although you should not sit ramrod straight and unmoving in the chair, neither should you allow overuse of gestures or mannerisms to interfere with your presentation.

**Posture.** Your physical bearing and posture sends an immediate signal to the interviewee when you walk into the room; so does the way you sit in your chair. The message you hope to convey is one of being somewhat relaxed and self-confident, without coming across as laid-back, overconfident, or cavalier.

**Facial expression.** People with a warm, natural smile have an advantage in any interpersonal situation. This is especially true in an interview. Not only does it convey self-confidence, but it also makes the interviewee feel good. You come across as a nice person who appears to be very interested in the person you're talking to. On the other hand, some people have difficulty smiling, especially "on demand." What should you do? Do not force it. You will run the risk of projecting insincerity.

If you are interviewing a potential candidate, chances are you'll check references before an offer is made. It is imperative you check references. Since recruiters and hiring managers know that job seekers are going to list only those references with glowing things to say about them, why has this drill become a hiring process standard?

Character references from friends and family members are no longer of little value to the hiring process. Letters of recommendation often make for better references than testimony via email or telephone. Furthermore, they could save both you and your potential employee time and energy. With letters, you will have written documentation of an employee's performance. If you have not done so already, it is not too late to go back and ask for letters from previous managers and associates. The reference list is aesthetically unassuming, commonly considered a formality, and often an afterthought to the resume and interview. However, when developed properly, it can be one of your most effective hiring tools. References can make or break the deal. A little forethought and preparation will go a long way in finding out whether or not someone is the right person for the job.

A company is only as good as its employees. How you handle the recruiting and hiring process determines the success or failure of your operation. So, if you want to enjoy business success, a step-by-step approach to hiring should be included along with your personal judgment skills and intuition.

## You Can't Chain Them to Their Desk

The problem with the majority of superstar employees, however, is they are easily lured away because of their talent and skills. Their absence leaves a void that is difficult to fill. So a challenge for you as business owners and management is to create a climate and environment conducive to longevity and loyalty. You need to retain your superstar employees. This is done by identifying the employees you want to develop and retain. Make every attempt to understand the qualities and behaviors that make them so valuable to your business success. Once you have identified them, work with those employees to create a developmental path and succession plan for their future. This could include putting them on projects that will give them more exposure, letting them participate in the policy decisions or product development, and giving them outside training. Many executives incorrectly believe that good compensation is enough to keep employees happy. This simply isn't the case; what superstar employees want more than anything is to be a part of something great while being appreciated for their contributions. Of course, they do expect to be rewarded for their hard work as well. Listed below are some guidelines for retaining superstar employees:

- **Communicate your vision of the company's future in such a manner that your staff feels a part of the company's goals and future. It's difficult to compete with a business that has a shared vision where all employees understand their potential for growth.**

- **Establish a culture of success. Reward your employees based on their performance. This helps to eliminate complacency. Link their accomplishments to compensation. One of the best methods of doing this is to offer a bonus to superstar employees who exceed the job expectations, then to those employees who meet the job expectations. Whether you're a small, medium, or large employer, pay competitively within your market. If you** can't pay competitively, provide other incentives that reward your employees such as flex time, vacation, and college tuition assistance for both themselves and their families. Also, consider giving your key employees equity in your company. This can be accomplished through a phantom stock program or other equity-sharing programs.

- Create an employee professional development plan. A structured career path and the compensation that accompanies the advancement motivate employees to work toward a goal. The way you can ensure this path forward is to have regular discussions regarding the employee's growth within the company. This will keep you in the loop with your key employees.

Every company desires talented individuals and will do what is necessary to bring them on board. To prevent your superstar employees from leaving, identify their key talents and find what motivates them, and then do everything possible to keep those superstars. You have far more influence over retention and then you might imagine. Your decisions, actions, and treatment of your employees determine who will walk out the door or stay for thirty years. Reach out to your superstar employees, empower them to make a difference, and help them to see how valuable they truly are to your company. By helping them to realize their importance and improving their careers, you are also making an even bigger difference in your own.

People leave managers, not companies, so before you promote your superstar employees to management positions, be sure they have or can develop good management and leadership skills. Provide regular management and leadership training to all of your managers. Research has shown that employees want their managers to know how to manage as well as be leaders of the organization.

Are you about to lose one of your best employees to the competition? Superstar employees set high standards for themselves and, spoken or unspoken, for the people who lead them. When their job isn't satisfying, they often become open to outside influences. So, understand that if your company lacks strong discontent and internal turmoil, superstar employees normally won't take the risk of leaving—often despite some very tempting opportunities.

If you want to retain your best players, you must invest the time and energy required to become their trusted mentor—to guide them, to draw out their real career concerns, and to help them feel a part of your company and appreciated. If you do these things consistently over time, you will have built a team determined to help nourish the growth and success of your business. Your investment in superstar employees goes well beyond retention of that one employee. You will also build a reputation as a company dedicated to their employees, which will consequently help you entice additional talented employees to join your team. This creates a win-win advantage for everyone involved.

In today's competitive environment, there is more pressure to succeed than ever before. Hiring and retaining superstar employees also comes with a new form of pressure. To ensure your company's success, you must look at future employees as investments, ones that will grow and benefit your company and work beside, not behind, you. Seek out those emerging leaders; train, educate, and develop them, for they are the future of your success.

## Action Steps

1.  Look at your current hiring techniques. What type of results have they brought you? Are there any more innovative methods you could incorporate into your hiring process?

2.  How many opportunities for cross-training are in your company? Identify them and see how they can improve your overall productivity and employee morale.

3.  Determine if your company establishes a culture of success. Do your employees want to stay and take a vested interest in the company?

# Chapter 12

Over the past eleven chapters, we've discussed how customer hospitality is essential for your company's survival. While there are many different types of businesses in this world, a common challenge they all seem to face is customer hospitality. Customers from all walks of life moan and groan about the treatment they receive by employees who just don't seem to care. While the global economy and the Internet have given businesses the opportunity to serve more clients than ever before, the trend has also given way to impersonal or, in some cases, nonexistent customer hospitality. With this knowledge in mind, why then do so many businesses today fail to realize that they are regularly losing valuable customers by not providing an exceptional customer hospitality experience?

Ninety-nine percent of people don't take a look at their own industry and say, "I want to be the most highly sought after person in this field, be recognized as an expert, and set the level of the playing field." But why don't they—specifically? Our professions are more than just jobs—they are our communities and cultures. What we do for a living provides a service to society. It doesn't matter if we are a top-level CEO or a frontline associate in a convenience store. We all should strive to do our best at any given moment. Our goal is to be leaders and set an example for those around us. Every profession has leaders. But often the thought leaders prefer to lead through writing and speaking, cutting-edge projects, and dialogue. Leadership means not just talking but listening, and not just vision but consensus. Leaders build a web of relationships within their profession and articulate their ideas to others. In a world of relentless innovation and change, every employee must be a leader.

Some people say, "Leadership isn't for me; I'm just an entry-level employee" or "I just want to do my job, collect my paycheck, and go home." Unfortunately the world doesn't work that way. As we mentioned earlier, we are more than just our jobs; we set an example for others. Leadership skills are essential for everyone in the workforce today because everyone's job is now the front lines. So the question is, how do we become leaders in our field? Leadership is more than just declaring yourself a leader. The process of becoming a leader doesn't happen overnight; it has to be taught.

Your Success Coach can teach you how to give your customers an exceptional experience on a daily basis. We incorporate training methods that build upon strengths, encourage continual learning, encourage striving for excellence, motivate to seek out life's passion, share with others, and pass along the experience. Your Success Coach helps clients unleash their capabilities and reach their infinite potentials. We are catalysts for change and provide options, perspectives, encouragement, support, and concentrated attention, giving the insight and confidence needed to move forward toward the accomplishment of your purpose, vision, goal, or objective. We can and will help you take the steps toward achieving defined goals by holding you personally responsible and personally accountable to yourself and the goal or objective.

To gain the full advantage of this learning experience it is very important to choose a company that is the leader in this field. Your

Success Coach has the knowledge and experience to help you build a strong loyal customer base, retain employees, and increase your bottom line. This is the experience level you will gain with Your Success Coach. This is the experience that will make customers come calling at your door.

Outstanding customer hospitality takes a negative and turns it into a positive that ensures the customer is not only happy, but has also just received an experience unlike any other and will forever remain loyal to that company. Results speak louder than words; we work with companies and individuals in getting desired results through many forms of learning. We are looking forward to working with each and every one of our customers to achieve the success they are looking for in life and in business.

As members of the National Speakers Association, we offer a wide variety of seminars to help you and your staff get your business on the right foot, including ones specializing in

- **Sales & Goal Achievement**
- **Leadership Skills**
- **First Class Manager & Leader**
- **Customer Hospitality & Loyalty**
- **Dealing with Difficult People**
- **Communication Excellence Skills**
- **Work & Life Strategies**
- **In addition to our extensive list of seminars, Your Success Coach offers**
- **Executive Training**
- **Personalized Training**
- **Package Suggestions**
- **Keynote Speaking**
- **Group and Individual Coaching**

Our goal with Your Success Coach is to make a positive difference in all the lives and businesses we touch. We are committed to aiding you in reaching your personal or business outcomes. Together, we can create enriching relationships where might is always done for right; and as Napoleon Hill states, "Whatever the mind can conceive, we can achieve."

With our training and coaching, we can give you the confidence to maintain positive-driven relationships with your clients, customers, and friends based on honesty, integrity, and most of all, respect. The training that Your Success Coach provides is a defining factor in the success of your desired outcomes: growth, prosperity, excellence. We focus our energy on your success. Your Success Coach can help transform your life, your business, and everyone you influence. You are the driver of the transformation process and we are your road signs and maps along the journey to your success. After working with us, you'll be certain of who you truly are, where your company is going, and what type of a difference you're going to make, and you will be able to change the lives of many by changing your own. All movements, advancements, learning, and actions taken on your part will show through your results and will impact others around you. As we always say about Motivation & Energy, "It's Contagious—Let Us Share Ours with You!" Your Success is Our Success! Wake up; the World is Yours! ™

For more information on Your Success Coach products and services please visit http://www.yoursuccesscoachbiz.com/index.html.

Changing people's lives through one great customer hospitality experience at a time!

*— LeAnne and Victoria*

# About the Authors

## LeAnne Williamson

LeAnne Williamson's steadfast vision of success has taken her from various upper level management positions in a Fortune 500 corporation to forming her own company, Your Success Coach. LeAnne has dedicated her life to helping others succeed by teaching companies to bring out the best in their associates through various training and coaching programs. Along with Your Success Coach, she conducts professional speaking to audiences across the country. Her passion for customer hospitality has helped companies rebound from the brink of disaster to unparallel success. Together, she and co-author, Victoria Bowring are committed to seeing your company succeed through specifically tailored programs and seminars. LeAnne is available for keynote speaking, breakout sessions, and consulting. Please email her at leanne@theyscgroup.com.

# Victoria Bowring

Victoria Bowring worked as a successful realtor earning several sales awards. She consistently ranked among the top realtors in her agency with annual sales upwards of $40 million. Spending the majority of her career in the field in customer hospitality, it was a natural fit for her to join the team at Your Success Coach. Her desire to see companies fulfill their potential is evident to anyone who meets her. She and co-author, LeAnne Williamson share a vision to help every business, large or small, maximize their revenue through customer loyalty. Victoria's innovative teaching style makes her seminars and personal and business coaching highly sought after by anyone who knows the value of customer hospitality. Victoria is available for keynote speaking, breakout sessions, and consulting. Please email her at victoria@theyscgroup.com.

Breinigsville, PA USA
22 June 2010
240401BV00001B/3/P